T0156586

The Other Side of the Tape

✦

Tales of Lunacy and Stupidity in Shipping

Joseph Willish

iUniverse, Inc.
New York   Bloomington

The Other Side of the Tape
Tales of Lunacy and Stupidity in Shipping

iUniverse books may be ordered through booksellers or by contacting:

iUniverse
1663 Liberty Drive
Bloomington, IN 47403
www.iuniverse.com
1-800-Authors (1-800-288-4677)

ISBN: 978-1-4401-1741-1 (pbk)
ISBN: 978-1-4401-1742-8 (ebk)

Printed in the United States of America

iUniverse rev. date: 02/17/2009

CONTENTS

Introduction

No business in the world works with the same levels of hatred and idiocy as the shipping business. It's the twelfth level of Hell; just passed jamming your thumb in a car door for eternity and being trapped in a cramped elevator with someone who has horrible gas for all time. When you walk into any typical store, you pay someone money and you leave with something. As soon as you get your purchase home, that's *your* stuff. You do with it as you please and no one else can play with it.

In shipping, you walk into a store and pay someone money to take your stuff away from you. That's *your* stuff! What's that guy doing with your stuff?! It's counterintuitive. You've just given up your money and your stuff to someone you don't know for it to zip through a process you don't understand to arrive at a destination you may or may not know anything about. Understandably, you're probably pretty pissed off.

The situation gets worse when you account for the motivations behind why people ship. Perhaps your stuff is broken and needs to be sent back, or you have some vital documents that you need to get to someone important. Well, since you're angry the item is broken or you're stressed about getting your papers there on time, your shipping experience will automatically be unpleasant for all parties involved. But you could be shipping for some happy reason: you're sending a care package to a son or daughter at college or it's a birthday present for your friend's new born baby. Either way, you still had to buy everything, get it into the car, lug it all the way to the store, wait forever in line, pay to have the stupid thing wrapped and put in a box, etc.

What makes the situation fundamentally God-awful is that you have to trust someone. Most people would rather chew glass than trust a stranger with their stuff. We've all had faith that a friend will return that book you lent them or bring back your car with a full tank of gas like they promised but they never deliver. And those people are friends! Now you're entrusting your stuff to a completely random person. Maybe certain people have little problem with that but they are few and far between, or penniless after giving out their credit card information. Either way, they rarely ship.

The average person who ships is like another person you'd encounter on a day to day basis: incurably suspicious, quick tempered, easily confused, and hopelessly lost. They believe that five minutes after they have left the store the people they have just entrusted with their stuff are now running around wearing their returned clothing, eating the care package they had sent to their son or daughter at college, and doing lines of cocaine off their precious family photos. While this would be hilarious to people in the shipping industry, nothing could be further from the truth. Peoples' things are safe for one important and unwavering reason; the professionals who ship a person's goods don't give a damn about customers, plain and simple.

Customers have no idea what they're doing. Shipping agents have a firm grasp of the process customers need to get through. However, since customers are stubborn and, let's face it, typical human beings, they will try to fake their way through the process as if they know what is best. Their obvious stupidity will spill out for all to see and they know it. And so people go on the offensive before they can be discovered as frauds, thereby saving their fragile egos. The people who ship things see this everyday. They understand and they can sympathize. However, once a customer has gone the typical route (and believe me, they will), they will be looked down on and despised. That is why peoples' stuff is safe; not because it isn't valuable, but because the people who ship shit are afraid that if they get to close to it, the customer's idiocy will rub off on them. Trust me, I know... I'm one of them.

It's important that you, the reader, don't take all this information personally. It's not healthy if you do. This diatribe is in reference to humanity in general. Sociologically speaking, an individual is an intelligent creature but it is the exposure to a group mentality that turns them into a drooling moron. People are conditioned to go with the flow and if the flow runs right into a brick wall, it's easier to go along with the group than to actively think for one's self. It's probably not something a person can pick up on. It's just something they've been conditioned to function with as members of a dysfunctional society. At least, I think that's what I learned from my utterly useless sociology degree. After all, I do work in shipping now.

For the better part of a decade, I've spent my days knee deep in corrugated cardboard, bubble wrap, and the soul-crushing despair of inter-state and international supply chain solutions. I've been with multiple companies, doing the same thing over and over again, and even though the faceless corporation might change, the difficulties, inadequacies, and raging stupidity always bubbles to the top. I should be bitter, and I am. The sheer depth of idiocy, selfishness, and human intolerance I have witnessed in the shipping industry has body slammed my once bright and chipper demeanor through the cheap folding tables of despair and hopelessness. Everyone feels that their job in some way kills a little part of them. But on the economic battlefield, shipping is the Gatling gun firing rusty nails dipped in hot sauce: it just stings a little more.

The process should be simple: hand me a box, tell me where it's going, and give me the money. Unfortunately, I have learned that nothing in this world can ever be that simple. Over many long days and nights, I have been witness to just how many special children this short bus we call a country really carries around. I have seen respectable business men fill out shipping orders in crayon. I've heard the unspeakably disturbing life stories of countless people answering the simple question, "What's in the box?" I've even witnessed mental breakdowns during the basic task of opening the door to enter the store. Seemed far fetched? I swear to you now, upon all that is holy and good in this world, everything I will tell you has really happened. Nothing has been embellished. No stories have been concocted. People truly are this stupid and crazy. If you still have a shred of respect for humanity, stop reading now. This ain't gonna be pretty...

THE MANY FACES OF SHIPPING

Everyone ships at some point in their lives. Ok, maybe not everyone. Hermits and shut-ins have little need for interstate commerce with the exception of infrequent deliveries of shotgun shells and lice shampoo to their shanties. But some hermits do ship. Just look at the Unabomber. The point is, at some point in a person's life, they will probably have to get their stuff somewhere and at that point they will fall into one of ten particular categories of shippers: The Ignorant, Speed Demons, Crab-walkers, High Rollers, Monologuers, TV Hags, Bubble Junkies, Re-Runs, In-My-Country's, or the Blessed Few. Bear in mind that people can incorporate elements from many of these categories, thus making them an even bigger pain in the ass than if they just fell under one.

THE IGNORANT

The Ignorant are by far the most common because they make up most of the population to begin with. It really doesn't matter that they are shipping as their idiocy follows them like the stench of death on a dog with the mange. These are the people that in any other store will accost a clerk, take up everyone else's time, and ask how much an item costs, despite it being clearly labeled in front of them. For our purposes today, their ignorance gets magnified a thousand fold when they hold a box in their hands.

Ignorants have no concept of reality. They wander in aimlessly and hopelessly try to accomplish a task they have no idea how to grasp. Many times, they will have no idea where their package is being shipped. As simple as that is, they just don't know where it's going. One would think that if they knew they had to ship something, and I mean they had gone through the entire set up process (they realized they needed to send something to someone, they found a box for it, carefully wrapped the item and sealed it with tape, carried it out to the car, got in and drove to the store, took the box out of the car, and walked in to ship it out) that they would remember, at the very least, the address it's going to.

They may have no idea what they are shipping. I don't just mean they have a problem describing the item to a shipping agent. I mean they literally don't know or don't remember what is in the box. If they packed it, they should know what's inside, even on the most basic level (food, clothing, toys, etc.). If they didn't pack it, how hard is it to ask the person who did, "What's inside?" In this modern world of terrorist paranoia, can anyone really be sure that if something is wrong with the package that they won't get in trouble for it? After all, they were the patsy that shipped it. Unfortunately, Ignorants never think that far ahead. They have no problem accepting when someone says to them, "Hey, do you mind shipping out this box of ammunition and dope... I mean this box of delicious cookies to my buddies in Afghanistan for me?"

It is even possible that they won't be able to answer the question, "Have you shipped with us before?" with either a yes or a no. They have no idea. It is beyond their mental acuity to figure out if they have ever, in their entire lives, been in that particular store and sent something out. How would you not know that?! Do these people only ship drunk or does packing tape induce some sort of black out? For most people, shipping is not an everyday experience so they should be able to recall an experience well outside of their day to day habits. If it *is* an everyday experience, then they should know if they've shipped before because they were in the stupid store yesterday!

Now, perhaps I'm judging them too harshly. It's conceivable that a good portion of these simpletons have Alzheimer's Disease or have recently suffered severe head trauma and it is an absolute miracle that they could even operate the door sufficiently to make it into the store (A feat that some really do have trouble with. That's right; some of them are too stupid to open the door. That's a story for a little later). But if this is the case, they shouldn't be wandering about trying to run errands. They should be carefully monitored to make sure they aren't a danger to themselves or others, which is what they become when they try to ship. And statistically, it would be impossible for so many people to be mentally deranged or hemorrhaging in the brain. They all drive to the store so car accidents would be in the hundreds of millions per year, and that's just in front of the building. The simple conclusion is that these people are just stupid; powerfully stupid.

They will tell you flat out, "I've never done this before," or, "It's been years since I've shipped anything." Nevertheless, their lack of knowledge doesn't stop them from becoming instant experts in interstate commerce. There is no need, in their eyes, to fill out a parcel shipping order, or PSO, with the vital information needed by the agent to get a package where it needs to go. Maybe they're illiterate, which I'm sure many of them are. But since they know exactly what is needed to complete a shipping transaction, they are in the perfect position to just "wing it".

Somehow, the agent is supposed to know where the item is heading. If Ignorants are asked, "Where is the package going?" agents will get answers such as, "To my aunt Gloria," "Down south," or even, "Well, it's not going there. It's going to a different place." I don't know Gloria, nor do I know where the hell she lives. If the only information I get is, "down south", I'll ship the damn thing to Peru just out of spite. And if it's going to a "different place," where was the first place it wasn't going to?!

Ignorants will generally not know their own information either. They can't remember their phone number or they just moved and have a new address they can't remember or they are shipping something for someone else and aren't sure if they should put their information or the other persons, etc. Damn it! Write down that you live in Candyland for all I care! All I care about is where it's going. Once I have that, you can return to your cardboard box or fortress of solitude. Whatever!

Example: A woman walks past the store three times, each time looking in the window and checking the sign. She finally comes inside and asked, "Do you ship things here?" despite the walls, doors, signs, and equipment being covered in the company logo of a very well known shipping company. She proceeds to inquire about a shipping estimate on an item going to another state. Of course, she can't remember which state so she'll have to come back later with the address. As she heads for the door, which she had stepped through no more than forty seconds ago, she makes a quick right turn towards the wall and begins to push on the solid barrier to get out. She has to be told the door is on her left and that she is pushing on a wall. She giggles and exits. (I swear to *God* this is a true story.)

SPEED DEMONS

Speed Demons are always in a rush. No matter what time of day or night, their package is the most important and it absolutely has to get to its destination before they even walked through the door. Of course, since their lives are so hectic, they simply cannot be bothered to give correct, or even complete, information on who they are, what they are shipping, or where it is going.

They will fly into the store, poorly-boxed parcel in hand and slam the item on the scale, even if the agent is dealing with another customer at the time. They will tell the agent, "I ship here all the time. All my information is in the system. Just bill me later," and try to fly right back out the door. If any attempt is made to stop the Speed Demon, maybe in the hopes of getting just a little more info on what the hell they want done with their box, they will sigh loudly, roll their eyes, and stomp back to the front counter. "Look, I'm in a hurry. It's all right on the box. I'm in here all the time; you should just know my information already!" When an agent looks at the box and see what looks like the garbled scratchings of an insane asylum inmate, naturally they will ask what the Speed Demon means. At this point, the Speed Demon will be so enraged that they have wasted 35 seconds of their precious time they will grab the nearest pen and in large, kindergarten-like letters scribble their name on the box again. Generally, at this point they will insult the agent's intelligence by saying something sarcastically like, "Can you read that?" or "Do you want me to spell it slowly for you?" By now, they have looked at their watch or cell phone numerous times and have come to realize that they are incredibly late for whatever pointless and backward-assed appointment they had to keep. That is when they ask to see a manager.

Let's just say, for the sake of argument, that you are the manager. They will tell you, "I come in here all the time and I've *never* had this problem before! What kind of people do you have working here?! I am never shipping with you again!" Let us dissect this statement, shall we? If the person does, in fact, come in "all the time", then they should have learned the first time exactly what kind of basic information a shipping agent needs to send off a package. Furthermore, if they go in there all the time and act the way they have just acted, it's a fair bet that they have given this speech more than once. They say that they have "never had this problem before." If that is true, then every other time they've attempted to ship, they've dropped off the package as they just tried to do now and it got shipped as far as the dumpster out back. The "kind" of people working in the shipping industry are generally understanding, but more importantly, they have been trained to do a job. That job requires certain things from the customer in order to reach the desired conclusion. Just as in any other job, workers crave input from the customer; otherwise the customer is wasting their time and trying their patience. If someone wants a Big Mac from McDonalds, they have to tell the cashier they want a Big Mac, or at least point to a picture of one and grunt. If someone wants to ship something, agents need to know silly little things like where the fuck its going! Finally, if they are "never shipping with you again," that is not a threat but a blessing. Thank you, kind sir or madam, for taking your bullshit elsewhere and pushing the buttons of some other shipping agent who may just snap on you and rip your hurried little head off.

Example: A regular customer who comes to the store to use our office equipment speeds in on a typical day. He is shouting into his cell phone in at least one of seven different languages. He dashes to the front and asks immediately if there are any faxes for him. If there are any, he grabs them and scurries off to the nearest desk to look through them, still yelling in Russo-Italia-Span-Jap-Chin-glish. When he finishes, he'll have to send some faxes out at which point he'll shove the papers in front of an agent and start reading off the number before they're anywhere near the fax machine. He won't wait for a confirmation. He'll ask how much, slam money on the counter and be out the door and in his car before the agent has reached for the last quarter. He's one of the good ones.

CRAB WALKERS

Crab walkers are the laziest group of shippers. They are the ones who make an exaggerated effort with whatever they are shipping, even if it can fit in a Chiclets box. They slump their shoulders, strain their faces like an old man on the toilet, and pretend to muster whatever strength they have to lift their awesome parcel. Of course, they fail, and then it becomes the shipping agent's social duty to step outside, into the cold and rain and snow, and help these feeble souls get their package through the door. Nine times out of ten, the box they have strained over weighs less than twenty pounds.

Naturally, there are people out there who do need some form of assistance. A quadriplegic isn't going to be able to lift anything, unless of course they have incredibly strong teeth.

Crab walkers are those people who can obviously deal with the weight of their own shipment but actively choose to make the shipping agent take time out of dealing with other people to walk outside, get their crap out of the trunk of their car, walk back over to the door, have the agent open the door themselves, and then take their crap to the scales. For example, a thirty-five-year-old soccer mom in heels holding a latte most likely has the strength to put down her Starbucks for a moment and bring her bag of Victoria Secret returns into the store. It doesn't matter to them that the other people who showed up to ship something are now incredibly pissed off at the agent for leaving to help someone other than themselves. All they care about is making someone lift their stuff. Is it really any wonder Americans are so fat?

Example: A man in his early forties parks his truck in front of the store. He gets out and makes an exaggerated limp to the tailgate. He opens it and reaches for his parcel like a small child reaching for the cookie jar. After a minute or so, he will appear to give up and look over at the door with eyes like a cartoon character that has just lost their mother. If he has seen an agent, he'll come in and ask them very nicely if they wouldn't mind giving him a hand. You see, he has this old war injury that acts up on cold days or hot days or sunny days or rainy days, and he just isn't as young as he use to be. Why, he's sure that the agent use to play varsity sports and were probably the captain of whatever crap the customer is spewing at the moment. The agent will head outside to get the box, easily remove the twenty five pound item from the truck and head back for the door. Of course, the customer's not there to open it because he's pretending to intensely study the copy machine's many wonderful functions. Once inside, the package is dealt with, money is exchanged and the transaction is completed. At this point, the man will lightly sprint out the door and spryly leap into his truck. The only explanation is that shipping is therapeutic and getting you to lift his stuff miraculously healed him.

HIGH ROLLERS

High-rollers know exactly what it costs to ship every item, in every weight and dimension, to every location on Earth and they will welcome in a cold day in *Hell* before paying a cent more. These sub-humans salivate over savings. No hissy-fit is too big to throw in order to get another fifty cents off their price.

The important thing to realize is these idiots don't understand that shipping prices are in a constant state of flux. The rise and fall of gas prices, differences in package weights and dimensions, the differences in distance between urban and rural areas, and even severe weather conditions all affect the bottom line on a daily basis. Just because someone looks up a price online for a shipment in no way means it will be anywhere close to what they will have to pay. Even worse, if someone calls an agent and gives them vague weights, dimensions, and destinations, the estimate they get will be completely wrong (and let me stress that word *estimate*!). None of this matters to a High-roller. Their price is right, the agent's price is wrong, and if the agent doesn't do something to reduce the total then they'll just take their package somewhere else, to which shipping agents everywhere would like to say, "Don't let the door hit ya where the good lord split ya, you penny-pinching jerk."

Remember, when a package is brought to a shipping agent, that person has been specifically trained in the shipping industry. They do this almost everyday. They do this for a living. When a person ships once a decade and remembers that the last time they sent their inflatable sheep for puncture repairs it only cost them a buck twenty nine, they should probably take inflation into account and not argue with the agent who knows a hell of a lot more than they do.

Example: A woman with a box of canned peaches and kitty litter comes into the store. She has been there before and makes her shipping history abundantly clear by informing the shipping agent that, "I do this all the time. I'm in the system." Her information is brought up, the destination is determined, the package is weighed and measured, and a final price is tallied. She will grasp her chest as if she is having a heart attack. "That is *not* what I paid last time! I ship to this address *all* the time! Why is it so expensive now?!" The shipping agent will patiently explain how prices are determined by weights, dimensions, and final destinations. They will explain that in a global economy, fuel prices fluctuate. They will explain that they have no idea what happened the last time but this is the price this time. The woman will express her dismay thusly, "You people just get off robbing customers, don't you?! Who the fuck do you *think* you are?! I ought to call your head office and get this place shut down! I cannot *believe* it is costing me seven whole cents more to ship these peaches and kitty litter bags than the last time! I'm going to the post office!" She will come back next month to repeat the process.

MONOLOGUERS

Most people enjoy a good conversation. What could be more rewarding than sitting down to a cup of coffee or a pint of beer and really getting to know someone on a one-to-one level? It's always good to make new friends, just not when a person is trying to ship something.

When a person answers the question, "What's in the box?" with the statement, "Well it's a box of cookies for my sister that I told her husband I would send because she just had kidney surgery and is starting to feel kind of down about her career in the pharmaceutical industry since she got the gout from a pig the last time she went to an emu farm in Iowa for a week-long seminary that taught her…", that is a Monologuer.

These are the people that feel strangely compelled to share every detail about their lives in a misguided attempt to provide simple information. All shipping agents care about is the Who, What, Where, and When. Why never, *ever* comes into the equation. We don't want to know. For the love of *God*, we don't want to know! We don't care that their cat ate a whole bottle of paprika and sneezed so hard it blew a hole in their favorite throw pillow and that is why they are sending it to be repaired. We don't care that the second-string short stop on their amateur baseball team broke his pinky toe in a drunken pissing contest and now he doesn't need the cleats they are returning. We definitely don't care, nor do we want to even imagine, that they're sending back their most recent shipment of adult diapers since that new all gravel diet plugged them up nice and tight. And we sure don't need to know that the last time they shipped anything, the Kaiser had just advanced on the beach head that their squad was forced to capture with nothing more than needle-nose pliers. No anecdotes, no memoirs, no knock-knock jokes, no personal reflections, no tearful flashbacks, no war stories, and no rambling tales designed to make someone bleed from the ears. We don't want to know… We just don't.

Example: An elderly man comes into the store to ship a birthday present to his grand-daughter. The agent asks him if he has ever shipped at the store before. The elderly man will answer, "Well, let's see… I think we did around Christmas time since we had to get the gifts to the grand kids in Virginia. That's where my son lives. He's in the military." The shipping agent will pretend to be interested and continue to try and get the rest of the required information. A line will start to form behind the elderly man. "Oh, it's going here," the elderly man will say holding out a scrap of paper, "but I'm not sure you can read my handwriting. Let me just get my glasses on… There we go. Alright, it's going to 437 Livingston Avenue; you know when me and Barb, that's my wife, got married back in '53 we lived just up the road from there in a little house that was built on an old mule farm…" The line will grow longer. The agent will ask to see the paper and type in the information themselves. They will get the rest of the information from their own tools and give the customer a final price. "Really? It's that much to send this? Well, that's the government for ya. You know, I saw on the news the other day that the Senate wanted to pass a bill allowing taxes on the sale of plaid socks. Where does it end, you know? Boy I tell ya, when I was about your age, the last thing the government cared about was socks! I remember I was in boot camp about to be shipped off to Germany and I couldn't get a fresh pair of socks to save my life!" The line will be out the door. Other customers will start to give up the hope of shipping their items and leave. A riot will surely break out soon. The agent cuts the old man off, asking if there will be anything else and giving him the total again. Eventually, the elderly man will pay. "Thank you so much for your help. You know, I go to the post office but they're always so rude there. That's why I come here because I never feel rushed". The customer directly behind the elderly man will have to be restrained from choking him to death.

TV HAGS

Out of all the vapid, misguided pinheads that wander into the shipping agent's world, none do more for America than the TV Hags. These are the women (always women, ages 40 and up) who spend all day, everyday watching the Home Shopping Network and buying all the useless crap they can get their hands on. These are the women who keep America's economy going.

It doesn't matter if it's a collection of ceramic gnomes or a macaroni picture of Jesus punching out Mike Tyson; if it's on television they will buy it. They buy so much trash that half of the time they won't remember what they are returning. One can only imagine the fire hazards their homes have become: cardboard boxes stacked high against the walls, piles of hideous sweaters growing out of the floor, pointless kitchen appliances plugged into every outlet, and enough cheap, gaudy jewelry to create a deadly prism, like a multicolored magnifying glass on a crowded ant hill.

Most of the time, they will hate what they have bought and so it has to go back. And so they ship, in bulk, almost everyday of the week. Without their incredibly irresponsible purchasing power and infinite free time, the shipping industry may shrivel and die.

Example: An elderly woman comes into the store with a stack of boxes. She will place them on the counter and inform the agent that she has more. After ten or twelve more trips to her car, the counter will be covered with boxes of various sizes and weights all going to the same place. When asked what is in each individual box, she will inform the agent as to what the item is and, more importantly to her, why she is sending it back (i.e. that sweater didn't fit right, that back massager doesn't work like it did on the TV, these ear rings looked better on Susanne Sommers, etc.). They will all be sent the cheapest way possible and to insure that, she will have a pile of coupons she will try to use, some of which aren't even for the right store. When the total is tallied, the elderly woman will pay with a huff and make a comment about how high shipping prices are these days. Higher price, however, will not deter her from buying more useless crap and she will be back in the next day to repeat the process.

BUBBLE JUNKIES

Those who are freakishly paranoid about how an item is packed for shipping are known as Bubble Junkies. While some level of protection is usually required for most items, this does not mean a shipment of cookies should be able to survive a tactical nuclear strike. A broken VCR being shipped back to be *replaced* does not need a dozen layers of bubble wrap to keep it safe. It's already broken! Would you put a cast on the broken leg of your cat after the cat was just crushed to death by a truck? I don't think so. A 50¢ stuffed animal doesn't need thirty dollars worth of packaging material to keep it safe, especially if it's being shipping in-state. An extra twenty pounds of newspaper and scrap Styrofoam wedged around a stack of documents only adds to the overall flammability of a shipment.

While the amounts are bad enough, Bubble Junkies have a nasty habit of watching the shipping agent pack their parcel. This is naturally understandable. After all, it's their stuff that's being packed. However, these are the people that will give tips on how best to pack their things and will bitch up a storm if it is not done their way. If they don't trust the people who work in shipping to pack their items, why the hell didn't they pack it themselves? Boxes and loose fill don't require an Indiana Jones-type expedition to acquire. Once again, the shipping agent does this for a living. They know a lot more about what happens during the shipping process than customers do so they're probably in a better position to know what kind of packaging a person's items need. In conclusion, Bubble Junkies are at a higher risk of getting slashed in the throat with a box cutter since they hover like birds of prey to make sure an agent uses plenty of packing peanuts.

Example: A person walks into the store with a laptop computer that needs to be packed. They inform the shipping agent that, "it is very fragile and expensive. Nothing can happen to it." Of course, the shipping agent had *NO* idea that a laptop was either fragile or expensive. We all live in caves. The agent will take the computer to the back for packaging. The Bubble Junkie will follow the agent past the front counter and into the Employees Only section, something neither the agent, nor the company's insurance agency, like at all. The Bubble Junkie will inquire as to how the item will be packaged, despite the very obvious displays of boxes, bags, bubbles, peanuts, and any number of other items all designed for parcel protection during shipping. It is almost as if the shipping agent does this for a living! The Bubble Junkie will watch the packing process intently, frequently giving pointers and helpful tips on how to better wrap their parcel. The agent will thank the customer for their painfully superior knowledge as their grip on their utility knife tightens. Before the box can be taped shut, the Bubble Junkie will ask for more packing material, which will require an entirely new box since the original will be unable to hold any more peanuts. The process will start over again. By the time the Bubble Junkie leaves, the agent will have a burst blood vessel in their eye.

RE-RUNS

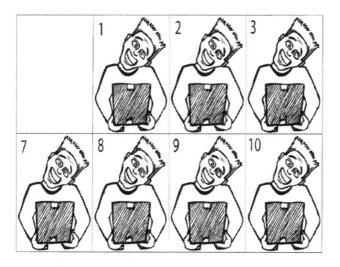

Re-Runs can cause confusion and deep depression if not watched for carefully. These are the people that come in everyday, usually at the same time of day, without regard to weather, holiday hours, etc., to ship the exact same thing to the exact same place. Nothing ever changes; the same items, the same weights, the same dimensions. One would think this would be a good thing for the shipping agent. The predictability and ease of processing should be a welcome change from the mass of unwashed retards that usually inhabit the store. Not so.

Re-Runs pose a threat on two different levels. First, they create an environment in which everyday is the same to the shipping agent. Repeat customers like this prevent the natural perception of the passage of time. If not watched for, a shipping agent will think that no time has passed at all and they are trapped in a perpetual time warp, doomed to spend eternity dealing with idiots and their boxes. Nothing is worse than feeling trapped in a job, unless the job is shipping.

Second, these bastards come in everyday with the same lame jokes and stupid mannerisms. Imagine hearing the same person, at the same time everyday, for years ask, "Hey, is it Friday yet?" or "How about this weather, huh?" Anyone would snap. If you were ever curious as to why postal workers went on killing sprees, I guarantee you a Re-Run had something to do with it.

Example: The same person comes in to the store at 5:37 p.m. again. They greet the shipping agent in the same way, again (i.e. "Hey there, sport!" or "Yep, I'm back again!"). They will expect some sort of chuckle or else they will try another painfully stupid joke. The agent will chuckle in a vain attempt to help save their own sanity. The Re-run will place the parcel on the scale and say, "same stuff going to the same place." The agent will run through the motions while the customer does whatever usual annoying habits they partake in while waiting to get through the shipping process (i.e. the will tap their nails on the counter, hum a stupid song, pretend to read the hazardous materials warning placard, stare in a very creepy manner at the agent, etc.). The agent will complete the process, take the customers money, and give them their receipt. The Re-run will say something to the effect of, "oh no, not another one of these!" They will chuckle again. The agent will have to chuckle in response. "See you again tomorrow," will be their parting comment as they walk out the door. The agent's soul will die a little more.

This band of rag-tag foreigners, with the twinkle of the American dream in their eyes, is one of the biggest pains in the ass a shipping agent has to deal with. This has nothing to do with race, beliefs, or general ethnicity. There is simply a problem with conversion. In their country, a package of hog knuckles weighing 67 clam shells and measuring 2,077 flibbertigibbets cubed cost 2 toe nails and a chicken skull to ship 35 pigmy-tosses down the road. *What*?!

With all due respect, this is America. Here, we do things a little differently. One of those things is business and if someone wants to do business in America, all parties need to know what the hell they're talking about. It's the same in every country. If I went to France to do business, I better learn the metric system and figure out how many francs I'll be making. It's all a matter of where a person is. But these customers get all pissed off at their shipping agent when they have no idea what the customer is talking about. Inches, feet, pounds, ounces, miles; these are the things agents are looking for. We cannot help you if your box weighs 80 marmot turds and needs to be shipped to Azerbaijan.

Furthermore, In-My-Country's have a concept of shipping in their country. Well, if they're *here*, then they are not *there*, are they? If a package is going to another country, it's going to cost a lot of money. It's no longer as simple as throwing it on a truck and carting it over to its final destination. There are customs departments to deal with and restrictions on items that can and cannot be shipped to certain countries. For example, used pots and pans cannot be sent to Iraq and no medicine can be sent to Nigeria unless they already make it there. International shipping laws are at the very pinnacle of insanity and a shipping agent has to deal with this all the time.

Another major problem is that now your package is traveling a great distance. There's logistics to be paid for; fuel for trains to get your package to planes or ships, freighting costs, distribution challenges, and the people paid to deal with all that crap. Is it really any wonder that it's going to cost fifty dollars to ship a letter to the other side of the world? Not only that, to guarantee that it gets there and within a certain, specific time frame? It's a miracle that letter doesn't cost a few thousand dollars. So unless In-My-Countries want to head back to the homeland themselves, parcel of hog knuckles in hand, they need to do the math to figure it out the American way and bitch to someone else about the price.

Example: A person walks into the store, without a parcel to ship. They will tell the agent, "I have package for making of the ship." The agent will have heard this phrase before and will immediately realize they're dealing with an In-My-Country. The agent will ask them where the item is going. They will name a country that has a population of twelve people and doesn't exist anymore. It is now up to the agent to try to give this person a price quote for the impossible. The agent will ask how heavy the package is. It will weigh .007456 kilo-ounces to the order of π. The agent will say its ten pounds. They will ask what the dimensions are. The In-My-Country will hold out their hands some distance apart. The agent will say its twelve inches cubed. Finally, the agent will ask, "What are you shipping?" The response will be, "Oh, is one of those, uh, things, uh, the, um, is a parrushioňiski. How you say in the Englished?" The agent will say it's a toaster. The final total will be somewhere around $500.00. The In-My-Country will ask, "Why so much?" The agent will tell them that to ship "something" of an unknown weight and unknown dimensions to a country that may or may not exist is never cheap. The customer will then ask, "Ok, what if I only shipping the one thing?" The agent will start to bash their own head against the counter.

THE BLESSED FEW

Once in a very, very rare while, a person of remarkable character and understanding will come into the store. They will have their items boxed and sealed with great care. They will have their information filled out in flawless detail with impeccable penmanship. They will answer all the agent's questions quickly and clearly with a smile that can brighten the room. And when the transaction is all set, they will be ready to pay, without bitching and moaning about the most recent fuel surcharge increase. They will pay, thank the agent for their help, wish them a pleasant day, and head out the door with no problems, no complaints, and a whisk of a fresh, clean linen scent. These people are known to shipping agents as the Blessed Few. I have yet to meet one.

Example: A being of pure light and beautiful energy will transcend the door and enter the store. Warm, loving vibrations will radiate throughout the building as they float majestically towards the counter. They will produce a box from the cosmos, perfectly wrapped, exquisitely taped, and nearly indestructible in form and function. Their box will be a triumph of engineering. Behold! Beautifully written, crystal clear paperwork is handed over. It looks as though it was penned by the gods themselves. The agent will input all the information and give this angel of mercy the final total. With a mere gesture, the exact amount is produced in flawless, freshly minted currency. Their receipt is handed over and they smile and say "Thank you." It is a smile that can melt the soul; the kind of smile a mother beams through tears as their child takes their first steps. Their thanks ring like a symphony orchestra. And suddenly, they are gone, filling the shipping agent with a void and a desire to see that customer once again. Or so the legend goes...

NO, YOU'RE THINKING OF THE POST OFFICE

A fundamental problem faced by anyone in the shipping industry is the common misconception that any company used to ship is just like the U.S. Postal Service. Well, it's *not. Ok*?! In fact, the major shipping companies are very different from the Post Office. The few things we have in common are that, like the post office, we move goods, we use street addresses, and if agents are pissed off long enough, we're likely to snap and kill someone.

First and foremost, the Post Office is part of the government. That's a big point. They are not a private industry and don't have to behave as such. Other shipping companies have to report back to them because, and this is important, they are the government. What makes a person think that if they can't ship something through them, they can ship it with someone else?

There once was a man who entered the store after just coming from the Post Office. He was already in a foul mood after he was told his parcel couldn't be delivered. He hustled in, threw the box on the counter, and glared at the shipping agent behind the register.

"I need to ship this," he growled.

"Alright," said the agent, "what's in the box?"

"I just came from the Post Office and they said to come to you."

"Ok, I still need to know what's in the box, sir."

The man's fingers began to curl on the counter as he took a step back. "Look, its only going upstate, ok? Why the hell do you need to know what's in it?!" he asked in a huff.

"Because there are restrictions on what we can ship and I can't send something if I don't know what it is," replied the agent.

The gruff man sucked at his teeth and thought for a moment. He let out a heavy sigh. "Alright, I'm sorry. It's just that this is really important to me and the Post Office gave me the run-around, you know? It's nothing dangerous. It's just some personal items."

"Sir, I need to know what's in the box."

"It's my wife."

The agent blinked. "I'm sorry, what?"

"My wife. I need to ship my wife."

"Your *wife* is in the box."

"Yeah, well what's left of her."

"Sir, we can't ship human remains or body parts. It's illegal."

The old man snatched the box off the counter. "Well what the hell am I suppose to do?! I don't want the bitch in my house no more!"

"Postage" is another point of contention within the shipping industry. Only the Post Office has postage. Everywhere else, it's know as, "pay us or your box will never move from this spot". Furthermore, the fees are going to be different from the Post Office. Shipping companies are private businesses that are out to make a profit for themselves. In private industry, a person pays for goods or services with prices that are set by an open and free market. They are able to go anywhere they would like to get the same goods and services at a price that best suits them. That's how capitalism works. So when one company tells a customer it's going to be a little bit more than the Post Office, it's perfectly legitimate to ask why. In the shipping business, the extra money goes to a guarantee of service: extra fees pay for things such as tracking numbers and insurance. With the Post Office, a person pays a few cents for a stamp and then wonders why their letter never got anywhere close to where they wanted it to go.

On multiple occasions, customers have waddled into the store with a package to ship and a predisposition on their mind. They throw down their box, neatly wrapped in craft paper and twine, and ask, "How much to send this Parcel Post to Klondike 5678?" or some such ancient gibberish. So begins the dance of the shipping agent and the clueless geriatric.

First, the shipping agent will inform the customer that only the Post Office does something called "Parcel Post" and that in the new millennium there are better, more efficient ways of moving goods. The customer will reply that in "their day" Parcel Post on a box of Werthers Originals only cost a nickel and the change got them two penny shows and free beating from a hobo.

Second, the shipping agent will inform them that their package can't be shipping as it is wrapped because the Pony Expressed died off years ago and their package with all its superfluous wrapping will get caught in a sorting machine and take a line worker's head off. The customer will reply that this is how they've *always* sent things through the Post Office, to which the shipping agent will reply, "Then why didn't you go there?" (Or at least, that's what they want to reply. Actually, it's a toss up between snapping back with that comment and smothering the customer to death with bubble wrap)

After this delightful exchange, the shipping agent with diligently repack the parcel, taking great care as the crazy customer watches over their shoulder, all the while complaining, "This is how they get ya on the price!" Information is gathered at an agonizing pace and put into the system. After all, why should the shipping company need to know the customer's address? It's not going to them, it coming *from* them! At the end of all of this, when the final price is tallied, may God help the shipping agent if the total should be more than the price of a stamp because, "That's not what it cost in *my* day!" About this time is when the customer asks if it's ok if they pay with a hundred.

Just because shipping and the Postal Service are similar does not mean they have anything to do with one another. For example, I honestly have no clue how the Post Office gets its pricing. I've heard it's based on everything from complex mathematical equations stemming from theoretical calculus to the fluctuating value of cow dung used in fertilizing the trees needed to make the paper for stamps. Who knows, but seeing as how they just started measuring packages instead of only weighing them, I'm pretty sure the rational can't be that complex.

The Post Master for any particular area and I don't regularly sit down to a cup of coffee and a game of Scrabble. In fact, I don't even know the name of the Postal Carrier that delivers the *store's* mail. I haven't set foot in a Post Office for at least two years because I have no need to. It's not that the people in the Post Office aren't nice folks; we just have very little time between us to get to know one another. As such, I don't know if the government uses lickable stamps to collect the DNA of the population. I don't know who designed the Postal Carrier's breezy short-shorts or what material they are made out of. I have no idea where someone can buy one of those bitchin' delivery cars with the steering wheel on the wrong side. And I don't know why the Post Office is closed on Sundays. I'm guessing it has something to do with Jesus.

"I want to mail this," an elderly lady said as she plopped her package down on the counter. "It needs to be there by tomorrow."

The shipping agent looked over the box and the address. "Have you shipped with us before, ma'am?" he asked.

"Oh, I'm not shipping it," she replied. "I just need to send it regular mail."

"Alright ma'am, but regular mail probably won't get it there tomorrow. It is going to Alaska."

The woman considered her options. "Alright, well how much is it for Priority Mail?"

"I wouldn't know, ma'am. I can only send it out Parcel Post and that won't get to Alaska by tomorrow. I can tell you what it would cost to send it using our Air service?"

"No, I just want to send it regular mail. How much for Express Mail?"

"I don't know."

"What if it's a Certified Package?"

"Ma'am, I don't know. All I can do is Parcel Post here. Anything else, you'll have to take this to the Post Office."

"Oh no, I much prefer it here. When will Parcel Post get it to Alaska?"

"I have no idea ma'am, but since it takes about two days to get a letter somewhere in-state, it probably won't be by tomorrow."

"Alright, when will it get there if I send it Priority Mail?"

The agent pinched the bridge of his nose to alleviate the pressure from his swelling brain. "Ma'am, I... don't... know."

"Well when will Express Mail get there?"

"Four weeks from next Tuesday!" the agent blurted out in frustration.

"Oh my, that's much too late. I'll just take it to the Post Office then."

TO DEFY THE LAWS OF PHYSICS

As you're holding this book, notice its weight. You can feel that gravity does in deed pull down on it at least a little bit. And it takes up space, not much but it does occupy some corner of this universe. It's a thing. Now what would make a person believe that this thing, with obvious physical properties, were somehow the creation of magical fairies sent from an enchanted forest, made of gum drops and wishes, and had the ability to weight nothing at all, take up less space than an atom, and make it to the other side of the planet in twenty minutes all for the same price as a local phone call? You guessed it: sheer stupidity!

When something is put in a box, it has a weight. That weight helps determine the cost to ship it. The more something weighs, the more it will cost: simple mathematics. But most things simple, and surely anything mathematical, are lost on the common idiot.

A severely disturbed and probably sexually frustrated man walked into the store one day. In his boney, money-hoarding hands, he held a small envelope with a simple address on it.

As he entered the store, nothing about his outward appearance really gave the impression that he should be viciously gang raped by rabid porcupines. That was only made apparent when he spoke.

"Alright, listen buddy. I don't want a lot of bullshit about this and I don't want you to waste my time or yours. I need to get this envelope to New York City by tomorrow morning. How much is it going to cost?" the rude man said to the shipping agent. Naturally thrown off by his incredibly rude nature, the shipping agent paused for a moment and asked to see the envelope. The man handed it over.

When he read the address, the shipping agent said to the customer, "Sir, we need an actual street address to ship this to."

Enraged, the man answered back, "What are you talking about? It has an address!"

"Sir, all this envelope says is that it's going to 'Madison Square Garden in NYC.'"

"Yeah. And?"

"In order for us to deliver something, we need a real street address. It has to say something like '123 Main St' for example."

"You're telling me that no one in your company knows where Madison Square Garden is?" the man said sarcastically.

"Are you saying that Madison Square Garden is so important that it exists in its own little world outside of normal shipping guidelines? We need to know which building, which department, which person; anything to get it to a specific destination. It's like shipping to the Hoover Dam: without any more information, one of our drivers will pull up and chuck it right over the side. Mission accomplished." the agent replied, just as sarcastically.

The man scoffed. "Just put it in the way it's written. And I want it insured for a thousand dollars."

"We can't insure this package," the agent said, once again sending the man into a rage.

"What do you mean you can't insure it?! These tickets are worth a thousand dollars! What if they get lost or stolen or something?!"

"To this company, they aren't tickets, they are pieces of paper. We do not insure any documents for their printed value."

"Fine! Whatever, just send them."

"To get them to 'Madison Square Garden' by tomorrow morning it's going to cost twenty dollars and the delivery time is not guaranteed."

"No," the man replied instantly.

"Yes, that is the price," the agent replied.

"No, that's too high. You have to do better."

"The price is what it is, sir."

"Well then I'll just go somewhere else!"

"The nearest post office is just down the street on your right," the shipping agent said eagerly.

The man huffed. "What is it then? Weight? The size?"

"All prices are determined by weight, dimensions, and final destination."

"All right, what if I take them out of the envelope?" And this is where it all started. For the next forty minutes, the man did his best to calculate and recalculate shipping costs, trying desperately to get the price to go any amount lower. He even whipped out his very own calculator to figure out tax percentages to find the best cost benefit between government income and time-in-transit. Of course, what he failed to realize, despite being told several times, is that all shipping agencies round up their weights and dimensions to either the nearest pound or inch. So if something weighs less than one pound, it gets rounded up to... anyone? That's right, one pound. His four tickets to Shitheads in Foam Rubber Costumes on Ice would cost the same as they were originally quoted. No matter what origami he attempted with the packaging or alchemy he attempted on the numbers, the man was unable to change the price. Finally, he vaguely admitted defeat.

"Alright," he said, "what was the cost again?"

"Twenty dollars," the shipping agent said, his hair a mess from being pulled at in frustration.

"Here," the man handed over the money and the transaction was completed. In an effort to avoid, "a lot of bullshit" and to, "not waste my time or yours," the man had spent nearly an hour arguing the cost of a package being sent to a place it most likely wouldn't be delivered to correctly in order to save what would amount to pocket change. He left the store and promptly got in his shiny new Mercedes and drove off.

What lessons can the good people of the world take from this inspiring tale? First, if a person wants to ship something, it has to be able to go somewhere. The jerk in the story wanted to send his package to a building in a city. That would be fine and dandy except for the fact that the system just doesn't work that way. If it did, then every yahoo would walk in trying to get their package sent to, "that guy in that place who did that thing that one time." Shipping deals in straight lines. In physics, Point A to Point B is your only option for a straight line. Point A to somewhere close to the suspected whereabouts of Point B isn't going to cut it.

Second, there is a system in place, designed long before customers walk into the store, with strict guidelines and regulations about how a price is determined. If a package weighs less than a pound, it will be rounded up to a pound. If a package weighs 2.5 pounds, it will be rounded to 3. If a package is 4.73245 inches in length, it's going to be seen as 5 inches. This is done to ensure enough space is available in cargo containers or freight cars to facilitate the maximum number of parcels their weights and dimensions will allow to be transported at one time safely. Believe it or not, that is what keeps shipping prices from being much, much higher.

Numbers don't lie, customers do. Printing documents on 20lbs regular paper instead of 28lbs laser paper won't save money on shipping. Removing one pair of socks from the box won't save on shipping. Distracting the shipping agent with mathematical bullshit won't save on shipping.

Finally, don't be a dick. Most shipping agents know enough about the system they are using to pull off little tricks to increase the price. The douche in the story was lucky enough to catch the shipping agent on what was predominantly a good day and so he wasn't screwed with too much. Most times, people aren't so lucky. Be polite. Say please and thank you. Customers that don't will end up taking a second mortgage out to pay for the shirt they're shipping back to the store.

A soccer mom, fresh from her trip to the Botox clinic, came in to ship one summer afternoon. The expression on her face looked as though she had either just woken up from a nap or was the butt of some sort of sarcastic joke. Either way, it was quite amusing to watch her talk.

"I need to ship these things," she said, her face a stoic monument to modern vanity.

"Okay, have you shipped with us before?"

"Yes, it's all going to my daughter at college. It's a care package." The frozen woman placed a large shopping bag filled with cookies and candies and extra pairs of socks on the counter.

"Alright then, I'll just go and box all this up."

"Oh, there's just one thing though," the woman said. "It can't be too heavy."

"I'm sorry?" the agent asked.

"My daughter just sprained her knee. She's on the basketball team and I don't think she'd be able to lift something that's too heavy."

The agent lifted the bag. "It's going to way about as much as this does now, ma'am. Just need to add on the weight of the box."

"Oh, that's too heavy for her I think. Is there anyway you could arrange the items so that it'll be a little lighter?" she said.

Due to the frozen expression, the agent really couldn't tell if the woman was joking or not. "Well, is there anything you could take out to make it lighter?"

"No, she needs everything. I know she can't live without those Twinkies! Hahaha!"

That was one of the creepiest laughs the agent had ever seen. "Ma'am, I can't just rearrange it to make it lighter."

"Oh well, I'm sure her knee's not *that* bad. But it might still be hard to handle. Is there anyway to make it smaller?"

The agent just starred as blankly at her as she did at him and then continued to the back of the store.

A frantic mother of some unbelievably annoying children hurried into the store one day. In her arms, besides her screeching offspring, was a small, worn box covered in scribbles. She set the child down, told both of them to be quiet to no avail, and turned her attention to the shipping agent.

"Hi, I need to get this to Florida as soon as possible," she said.

The shipping agent put in all the necessary information and told the woman, "Ok, the soonest we can get it there is tomorrow morning by 8:00 a.m."

The woman looked baffled. "You can't get it there today? I was told you could get it there today?"

"I'm sorry ma'am, but the soonest we can get it there is tomorrow morning."

"Well this is just great! I came all the way out here and my father needs his medication now!"

"I'm sorry but this is the best we can do."

"Why can't you get it there today?" she asked over the screams of her kids.

"Because we don't offer same-day service. Only private couriers do that."

"I was told that you do! My father needs this medicine by five o'clock!"

"Ma'am, it's 4:30. Even if we did offer same-day service, there is no possible way to get anything from here in New Jersey to Florida in half an hour."

"Well this was as soon as I could get here! I had to pick up the kids at school and take them to Gymboree and soccer practice and then get the dry cleaning and-"

"Ma'am, can't he go and get his prescription filled at a local pharmacy in Florida?"

"I don't know! I don't know anything about what he's taking! My father just told me it was incredibly urgent and he needed it there before five o'clock tonight."

"If you don't mind me asking, what's special about tonight?"

"It's my parents' anniversary."

"What's the medicine called?"

"Something with a V."

"Viagra?" the shipping agent asked with a grin.

"Yeah, I think so."

"Don't worry, ma'am. I'm pretty sure this shipment can wait until tomorrow."

Shipping agents can't bend time. While we are pretty damn cool, it's just not one of our amazing super powers. I can't get an "unbelievably important" shipment of stale bread crusts and belly button lint to Melbourne Australia in the next fifteen minutes. I doubt I'll be able to get it to the back of the store in fifteen minutes. I'm a busy guy. If it's in town, less than five minutes away, and I have some free time and a set of wheels, I may tell a person I can deliver it the same day but it will take a few hours and cost a lot of money for the trouble. Of course, someone can always hop in the car and drive it there themselves, but if they're stupid enough to take me up on the offer, they probably shouldn't be driving in the first place.

Conversely, I can't make the shipping process slower. It's not as simple as hitting the pause button and advancing the world one frame at a time. If I say that this service is "the slowest and the cheapest", I can be taken at my word. That's as slow and as cheap as it gets. Heading over to the distribution center and hobbling all the line workers might make it slower, but it won't be any cheaper. Getting in the car and hand delivering a package might make it cheaper, but since the middle man has been cut out, it won't be any slower.

An elderly man, decked out in groovy suspenders, cargo shorts, and knee high socks came into the store on a Monday morning. He just looked like an asshole, you know? He looked like the kind of guy who would strangle a puppy in front of a group of kindergarteners just to "let'em know what the *real* world is like!"

"I need boxes," he said matter-of-factly.

"Alright, what size do you need?" the agent asked.

"Something I can fit a three-ring binder in. That's all I need, you understand?"

Oh, the agent understood. He understood that this guy was getting charged double already. The agent went to the back and found the box closest to the size he needed and brought it out to show the dip-head. "Does this look like about what you need?"

"Yeah, that'll work. Ok, I need to ship this out then. Here's the address. Give me the slowest and the cheapest service you've got. I don't want to pay anymore than I have to."

"Alright, our standard service will get it there on Wednesday for $9.00."

"$9.00? Isn't there anything cheaper?"

"Nope, this is as slow and as cheap as it gets."

"What if it gets there later than Wednesday?"

"This is the slowest service we offer. It's just not going very far."

"Your competitor can get it there on Thursday for $8.50! Why can't you do that?!"

"I don't know, sir. I work for *this* company. This is the cheapest and the slowest we can do."

"But your competitor is cheaper! Why can't you guys just go slower?!"

"Why don't you just go use their service then?"

"Because then I'd have to cross the street! You should be able to move slower!" With that, the crazy old bastard left in a hurry. (Just a quick side note to this story: This guy came back a few times, each time causing a huge commotion about prices and time tables. When he was told to take up the issue with my boss, Daria, he said, "I don't deal with fuckin' women!" My other boss, Daniel, gave me permission to "beat the living shit out of him," the next time he came in. Now *that's* job satisfaction!)

PRICELESS CRYSTAL WRAPPED IN NEWSPAPER

It would make sense for a valuable item to be handled with great care. Works of art should be wrapped in plastics to protect them from air and the occasional scratch. Porcelain vases should be covered in many layers of bubble wrap and sprinkled liberally with packing peanuts. High tech computer parts should be sealed in anti-static bags to keep them from becoming worthless silicon door stoppers. It's really just common sense, but as is the way in the shipping world, common sense among customers was run over by an eighteen wheeler a long time ago.

An elderly woman walked into the store on a busy shipping day. In her feeble grasp was a box that looked as though it had been devoured by a garbage disposal. She placed the pile of cardboard on the counter and turned to the shipping agent.

"I need to get this to my daughter in New Mexico," she said in a sweet voice.

The shipping agent took one look at the box and refused to touch it, for fear it would turn to dust before his eyes. "Ma'am, whatever is inside is going to have to go in another box. This one will never survive the trip" said the agent.

"Oh no, I've shipped things in boxes like this before and they always arrived just fine. Besides, it's not very fragile."

"Alright, what's in the box?" the agent asked.

"It's my collection of glass figurines from around the world."

The shipping agent blinked in disbelief. "Ma'am, that's incredibly fragile. If you're going to ship with us, the items absolutely have to go in another box."

"No, I don't want to pay for another box!" the old woman said in a huff.

"Well then I'm sorry ma'am, but we just can't accept such an obviously damaged parcel."

"Fine then! You just lost a sale, young man! I'll take this to the Post Office!" the old woman said and snatched the box back off the counter. As soon as it cleared the edge, the bottom of the box gave way and her figurines came crashing down onto the hard carpeted floor. Without missing a beat, the old woman shoved a boney finger in the agent's face and said, "You're paying for that!"

At the other end of the spectrum are the incredibly paranoid. Certain items don't really need a few hundred feet of packing material to keep them safe. A collection of used Q-tips and stale underwear barely require a plastic bag, let alone a double-walled box.

Early in the morning, two large men struggled to get a box through the door. They made it up to the scale and gingerly placed the item down, like a new mother lays her baby down to sleep.

"This needs to be put in another box. It's extremely valuable and needs to be as protected as you can make it. I don't care what the cost is," one of the men said to the agent.

"Ok. What's in the box?" the shipping agent asked.

"It's motorcycle parts. Very delicate" the other man replied. Two shipping agents dragged the item over to the packing area and began the arduous task of wrapping the box itself in bubble wrap and then carefully placing it in an even bigger box lined with packing materials. After a half an hour, the two agents brought the item back out to the scale, which showed that the weight of the item had doubled since the new packing.

"Alright," the shipping agent said. "How much would you like to insure the package for?"

"Forty thousand dollars," one man said.

"Ok, and just for our records, what exactly is in the box that's now in the box?"

"It's an engine block."

"So basically, it's a large, nearly indestructible chunk of metal?"

"Basically," a man said. Both agents gave each other a look of disbelief.

"I see, well it looks like your finally shipping charge with all that insurance is going to come to just under two thousand dollars."

"Wow," said one man. "How much is it without the insurance?"

"About three hundred dollars."

"Well, put two hundred dollars worth of insurance on it and send it out like that."

Sometimes a shipping agent's finest efforts will be brushed aside as if they don't matter at all. They can meticulously wrap fragile items, even going so far as to demonstrate to the customer the various layers of protection they use in order to take every measure possible to ensure the safe shipment of the item in question. It still won't matter. They'll get blamed for something.

An elderly woman with a pleasant disposition came into the store on a sunny winter day. In her hands she held a shopping bag. In the shopping bag was a mystical artifact with the power to turn this seemingly chipper grandmother into a she-beast from Hell.

"Hello," she began. So far, so good. "I need to ship this out so that it will get there tomorrow." She placed the bag on the counter and took out the contents. It was a pillow. There was nothing particularly special about the pillow. It was like a million others one could simply pluck off the shelf at JC Penney's for about five dollars and throw to swiftly decorate a couch. Nothing special at all.

The shipping agent took the pillow into the back area to package it; something that should have been the picture of simplicity. After all, it's just a pillow. It's not going to shatter, crack, fracture, or burst into flames. A plastic bag and a suitable box should suffice. How wrong the agent was.

"Excuse me! You're not going to put it in *that* box, are you?" the elderly woman suddenly shrieked.

The agent was a bit stunned. "Yeah, the pillow will fit fine in here" the agent replied.

"No! No, I can't allow that! Give it back to me; I'll just go somewhere else! This is ridiculous!" The old woman's arms flailed as she motioned to get her pillow back.

"Ma'am," the agent said, "this box will work fine. If I use a bigger box it will be more expensive to ship."

"Use a bigger box then! It needs lots of packaging! It's very valuable and I can't have anything happen to it! If you use the smaller box, it could get crushed or punctured or… Just give it back to me! I'll take it elsewhere!"

"Alright, ma'am. I can put it in a bigger box."

"Fine!" the old woman said with a frustrated sigh. Having been rudely told how to do his job, the agent decided that the old hag was right. The pillow *did* need a bigger box. The agent reached for one usually reserved for entire wardrobes, televisions over 30 inches in length, and large engine parts. He diligently wrapped the pillow in bubble wrapped and filled the enormous box with packing peanuts. In total, the vicious old hag spent roughly $85.00 in packaging and service to ship one pillow, a fluffy unbreakable pillow, from New Jersey to New York City.

She came back in the next day to do the same with a blanket.

Other times, the agent will be faced with a shipper who is so specific in their packaging requirements one has to wonder why they just didn't pack the thing themselves.

A fat man with a wheeze shuffled in one day with something that was already in a box. It should have been an easy transaction at that point, but it wasn't.

"I need what's in here repackaged" the tub of goo said.

The agent took the box into the back and cut the tape to open it. As soon as he did, an explosion of packing peanuts, crumpled newspaper, and bubble wrap burst out of the box. The agent dug deeper to find the actual item being shipped and discovered it was a common clock radio. Why this large man thought it was necessary to bury this dime-store alarm clock in a mountain of protective material was unclear. Why the agent was being made to repackage something that had no risk of being broken, even if it was shot at, was unclear. So the agent pushed the mess aside and started to wrap the item in bubble wrap again.

"No, you're doing it wrong!" the fat guy yelled. "It has to be surrounded by padding and put in one box and then *that* box needs to go in another box filled with padding but you need to press down on the padding so that it's tight enough and stays rigid. You have to press down on the packing peanuts. I do this all the time!"

"Sir, if you do this all the time, why didn't you just package it yourself?" the agent asked the obvious blob as politely as he could.

The man huffed in annoyance. "Because you're supposed to be the professional packaging guy! That's why I brought it here so do it right!"

"Sir, I'm following standard packaging guidelines for a non-fragile item."

"It's fragile! It can break!"

"Things like crystal, china, and porcelain are considered fragile in shipping. A clock radio is not."

"Look, just pack it the way I said or I'll be talking to your boss about getting you *fired*!"

The agent packed the stupid little radio the way the man wanted it. Mr. Tank Butt was charged three times what the work and materials were worth for being an asshole. Unfortunately, he came back the next week with a stereo.

SHIPPING LABELS IN CRAYON

Like most shipping agents, I do not have a degree in dead languages. I have never decoded the Dead Sea Scrolls during my days off. I've never been prompted to decipher hieroglyphics on a lunch break. My co-workers and I generally don't chat about last night's baseball game in Aztec. That being the case, what chance is there that I, or any other shipping agent, will be successful at picking through the car wreck of atrocious handwriting that gets put in front of us?

There are, sad to say, dozens of times a day when a shipping agent will stare deeply at a shipping document trying desperately to determine if an "L" is an "I", an "O" is a "Q", or even worse if an "R" is a "Z". Numbers melt into letters, street addresses look like the T-wave on an electrocardiograph, zip codes contain too may or too few numbers, whole sentences are viciously crammed into the quarter centimeter boarder of the page, and even the names of the customers doing the shipping look like their pen had vomited onto the page. These are grown men and women. Elementary writing courses begin in the first grade. These people have had decades to develop their writing skills and most of the time the shit that spews out onto the paper doesn't even look like English.

I can understand the idiosyncrasies of penmanship. Everyone is a little bit different and so their writing style is going to vary compared to other people. And in today's type-written world, where high school grammar teachers actually encourage text messages to young cell phone users as a way to "promote and enhance writing skills", it is easy to loose touch with the finer style of the handwritten language. But English is a language we all seem to agree on, and there are rules for the written exchange of information from one person to another. So unless I witness a customer getting mercilessly beaten in the skull with an aluminum baseball bat seconds before they put their information down on the page, there is absolutely *no* excuse for forgetting what the letter "A" is suppose to look like.

On a breezy spring day not too long ago, a dashing businessman in a full three-piece suit proudly made his way into the store. His conversation rang out clearly as he spoke with authority into his Bluetooth headset. He walked confidently up to the counter and placed an envelope in front of the shipping agent.

"I'll have to call you back in a minute," the upright business man said and hung up his phone. "Hi," he said as he turned his attention to the shipping agent. "I need to send this out so it gets there tomorrow."

"Ok," said the shipping agent, "have you shipped with us before?"

"No." the man said.

"I'll just need you to fill out one of these then. It's your information at the top; Section A is where it is going, and then just sign at the bottom."

"Got it," the man said. At this point in a movie, the background music would have turned sinister.

A few moments passed and the man paused, looking puzzled. "How do you spell 'avenue?'" he asked. "My brain's just not working right today, I'm sorry." The agent said that was alright and told him how to spell the word. A few more moments passed and the man looked up again. "I'm sorry, how do you spell 'Philadelphia?'" he asked. The shipping agent understood: everyone has an off day and "Philadelphia" is a somewhat tricky word. Again the agent helped him and he continued to write on the shipping order. Then he asked, "How do you spell 'department?'" Now the agent was beginning to suspect he was illiterate and asked to see what he had put down on paper, just in case the address could be inferred from the context of the rest of the order.

Upon beholding the tangled mess of writing, the shipping agent could not find the words "avenue", "Philadelphia", or "department" anywhere on the page. All that could be seen was a horrible stain of brutalized letters and the angry scribbles of a potential madman. The shipping order was completely useless.

"Where is this package going?" the agent said bewildered.

"It's going to Philadelphia General Hospital's department of cardiology," the man said matter-of-factly.

"What exactly is in the envelope?"

"Oh, its chest x-rays of one of my patients. She under-going heart surgery later this week and it's important the surgical team gets these."

The shipping agent's jaw dropped. This man was a doctor in charge of a person's life on the operating table and he could barely spell his own name. The agent took a deep breath and continued with the transaction.

"Ok, Philadelphia General, right?"

"Yep."

"They have a good cardiology team?" the agent asked, in case he had a heart attack while shipping this package.

"One of the best. I should know. I was in residence there." The agent stopped worrying about a heart attack and focused on the impending embolism in his brain.

Another dapper, finely dressed gentleman walked into the store one day, intent on shipping a package. He placed the parcel down on the scale and smiled at the shipping agent. "Have you ever shipped with us before?" the agent asked.

"Nope," the man replied.

"Ok, I'll need you to fill out one of these," the agent said and handed the man a shipping order form. He explained what information went where and reached for a pen to hand the customer when he noticed the man reaching into his inside jacket pocket.

How he got them, the shipping agent didn't know. Why he had them, the shipping agent didn't want to know. The agent just stood and watched this grown man as he took a handful of Crayola Crayons out of his pocket and began to fill out the shipping order. The only thing that made the situation stranger was when he finished the section on his information and switched colors to fill out the destination.

I'LL JUST WALK THIS OVER FOR YOU

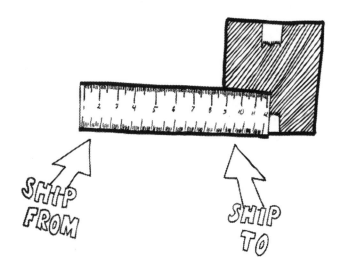

In the global scheme of things, interstate commerce is fairly low key. It takes far less effort to send something to Nebraska than Nairobi. It takes even less time and energy if something is being sent in-state. All it takes is to send it to distribution and it goes on a truck to its destination. No big deal. That is why most standard (non-express) shipments through any major carrier will get to where they are going the next business day if it's being shipped in-state. It's just not a big distance.

However, there are times when the distance is so extraordinarily small one has to wonder why the hell these people don't just deliver it themselves. Is the paper trail for the package that important? Does it look more professional to have it delivered than simply dropping it off? Can any human being really be that stupid and/or lazy as to have something shipped to a final destination literally a few dozen feet from where they sent it out? If I beat these people to death with a stapler, would I go to prison or be given a medal for protecting society from their idiocy? These are the questions that have plagued shipping agents for years.

A man walked in to the store late one night. He was tall, neatly dressed, and walked with determination and purpose. He appeared to be the very personification of a savvy, well educated man. That is what he *appeared* to be.

"I need to get this to its destination by tomorrow morning," he said in a pleasant demeanor.

"Alright, where is it going?" the shipping agent asked.

"Here," the man said and handed the agent a scrap of paper with an address on it.

The agent read it a few times, just to make sure his eyes weren't playing tricks on him. Finally he asked the man, "Sir, you do know that this address is in town, right?"

"I know," the man replied.

"In fact, it's the next building over."

"I know."

"Wouldn't it be easier to just deliver it yourself?"

"I'm not going to be around tomorrow morning."

"Oh, so you just need it delivered by a deadline because you'll be out of town, right?"

"No, I don't get into the office until noon."

The shipping agent's head began to hurt. "So, you want to spend about twenty five dollars to get this package next door by tomorrow morning because you like to sleep in?"

"Do you take Visa?" he asked without missing a beat.

The shipping agent's head began to pound. "In fact, I'm pretty sure they have a mail slot you can just drop this in. Why don't you just take it over there now?"

"I want to make sure someone gets it."

The shipping agent started to feel faint.

A woman came into the store one rainy fall afternoon. Her tiny umbrella did little to save her robust form from the deluge outside. Soaked from head to toe, she was obviously upset with the weather situation. She shuffled over to the front desk, shaking water droplets as she moved, and plopped an envelope down on the counter.

"Here, it's all ready to go," she said, referring to the shipping waybill attached to the front of the parcel.

"Ok," the shipping agent said. "Would you like a receipt?"

"Fine," the woman replied. At this junction, the shipping agent began to type in the small amount of information needed to process the package. Date, check. Account number, check. Type of waybill: Second Day. Destination: the next town over. The process came to a sudden halt.

The agent took a closer look at the envelope, thinking it was just a misprint. He read it again; maybe his eyes were finally going bad.

"Is there a problem?" the dripping woman asked.

"No, no, it's just that this seems to be going to the same address it's coming from," the agent said with a chuckle. The woman didn't react. He read it again:

Ship From: 124 Farthingtown Blvd, Floor 1.

Ship To: 124 Farthingtown Blvd, Floor 2.

"So you are shipping this to yourself?" the agent asked, blankly starring at the woman.

"It's going to the office above me," she said sharply.

"Why don't you just take it to them yourself?"

"Elevator's broken."

"Maybe that's why you're such a fat-ass," the shipping agent thought. "Why is it going Second Day then?" he actually asked.

"Huh?" Jabba the Dripping Hut answered.

"Standard service would get it there tomorrow for a lot cheaper. This waybill will get it there two days from now for about twice the price. Why are you sending it Second Day at a higher rate to get it there late?"

"Just give me the damn receipt!" she shouted. The agent handed her the completed transaction slip and watched her waddle away. At some point during the conversation, she had forgotten all about her umbrella and wandered back out into the rain. With her un-deployed umbrella tightly in her grasp, she made her way into the stormy parking lot and to her car.

An ordinary man came into the store. He came in to ship a letter to himself in Florida. Ok, fine. Apparently, it was going to his office and he'd be there to receive it. Ok, fine. Nothing about this made sense as he mentioned in passing that he, "hoped someone was at the office to sign for the letter." He paid nearly thirty dollars to get it to himself, meaning the name of the recipient was the *same* name as the sender, despite the fact that papers are not that difficult to carry on a flight he said he was taking to Florida later that day. Ok, fine.

Three days later, the same envelope arrived back at the store, the words "Refused By Recipient" stamped in large letters across the front. The reason for the refusal, also in large letters, was "Unknown Recipient". Apparently, either no one at this guy's office knew who this guy was or, even worse, this guy forgot his own name. I'm betting on the latter.

HOW TO SHIP DYNAMITE, LIQUOR, AND WEED

It would seem as though good judgment disappears from the average person's brain the moment they need to ship something. One minute they can distinguish between right and wrong, safe and unsafe, and even up and down. However, if a box is put in their hands, it is as if the merciful angel of good judgment got cracked in the head with a shovel, tied to a pick up truck, and dragged down a dirt road by the powerful goblin of ignorance.

There are two categories of stuff that can't be shipped. No one is special enough to get away with this crap. The two categories are essentially "stuff that's rare" and "stuff that explodes".

The first category is simple enough: if it's rare enough to be irreplaceable, don't ship it. The Crown Jewels of England and Einstein's brain are never shipped through regular means for a reason. Basically, this is a way for shipping companies to avoid horrendous lawsuits for incompetence, acts of God, or other unforeseen events that will surely destroy or misplace whatever piece of the Shroud of Turin someone might try to get to their summer house in Georgia. Accidents happen everyday. When the swallows return to Capistrano, there's a good chance they can get sucked into the jet turbine of a delivery plane and then a customer's package is just one of a thousand pieces of flaming wreckage. It can't be helped and it can't be foreseen. If a person doesn't want to take that chance with their priceless collection of antique rectal thermometers, they shouldn't try to ship them.

This includes non-monetary items as well. For example, grandma can't be shipped to her final resting place. There are specific laws and procedures for doing that kind of thing and a local mortician can be contacted to help with that. But I'm sure as shit no going to bubble wrap Granny's torso and cram her into a double-walled box. In fact, no agent should be asked to ship any part of Grandma. Organs and tissues are considered a biohazard and, more importantly, packing tape doesn't cling to them very well when they're still gooey. Another good example is pets. Little Fluffy is one of a kind. No one would want anything to happen to little Fluffy that might upset or injury it. Well, if someone wants to ship little Fluffy, I'm afraid Fluffy is going to have to be killed, disemboweled, stuffed with fire retardant chemicals, and freeze dried. This will no doubt take some of the playful nature out of Fluffy as it is hard to fetch anything when your organs are rotting in a medical waste bag heading to an incinerator.

Finally, there's money. No one should be foolish enough to try to ship money. That's just begging to get screwed. If someone wants to do that, they might as well wander through the slums of Mexico City wearing nothing but a muumuu of twenty dollar bills because the same thing is going to happen: they'll get robbed and if they protest, they'll get raped.

The other category, "things that explode", is the more serious of the two. These are the items that, if shipped and something goes even slightly wrong, the average citizen becomes a mass murderer. Gun powder has no place on a passenger airliner and it has no place on a cargo plane either. The job site being demolished in a few days will just have to be patient for someone to hand deliver the dynamite because I'm not touching it. And I'm sorry, Little Timmy, but your Uncle Joey will just have to wait until the next time he come to visit to see your awarding-winning science fair project of corrosive acids and homemade C4.

The little things count too. A junky sobering up in a half-way house can find matches for stolen cigarettes on his own so no one needs to ship matches to them. Even in the darkest corner of the world, grocery stores still sell bleach so that doesn't need to be shipped. Remember when you were a kid and you held a lighter to a can of hair spray and made a little flame thrower? Well, those things still work like that so they can't be shipped. Even perfume and cologne are flammable substances and shouldn't come anywhere near a delivery truck. I know many people say, "But I had it delivered to me! Why can't I ship it out?!" The cold, hard truth is that those people are idiots and if the dirty socks and stale Pop Secret they crammed in the box to protect the bottle fails, which it will, that brilliant shooting star across the night sky will be the plane their crappy, leaking package lit on fire.

Which brings me to a major point: alcohol can't be shipped. I'll repeat that. Alcohol cannot be shipped. Period. Here's a free history lesson: back in olden days, liquor was made wherever there was a still. Its value was based on how high the percentage of alcohol was in the mixture and was tested before someone purchased it in any quantity. To test its quality, the liquor was mixed with gunpowder and lit on fire. If the powder burned, the alcohol was strong enough, if it didn't light, the alcohol was too watered down. Therefore, if it lit, the booze was said to be "proved", which is where we get the designation "proof" to describe the percentage of alcohol by volume. In other words, alcohol burns. Hey, how about that!

Of course, it makes sense to keep dangerous substances out of the shipping industry's hands to begin with. We've all gotten boxes delivered to us and I'm sure everyone has seen the state some of them arrive in. Shipping is not a gentle process. Boxes are hurled, stomped, kicked, smashed, crushed, and run over on a daily basis. If something is sensitive to that kind of punishment, then there is a very good chance it will go off, taking with it whatever happens to be around at the time. Drivers and sorters understand the risk but explaining to the other angry customers why their items were detonated is a hassle I really don't want to deal with.

A man who was obviously convinced that New Jersey was part of the western cattle ranching portions of the United States moseyed on into the store one afternoon. In his possession were two boxes. He set the boxes down on the counter, adjusted his ten gallon hat, and greeted the shipping agent.

"Afternoon. Need to send these back to their manufacturers." His mustache danced as he spoke.

"Alright sir, what's in the boxes?" the agent asked.

"Well this one right here is some ammunition I ain't gonna use. That one's goin to Michigan I think."

"Sir, we can't ship ammunition. It's a hazardous material."

"But I got it shipped to me. How come I can't ship it back?"

"Because we would need a specific hazmat license to ship bullets. The company you ordered these from most likely has that kind of license."

"Shit! Now what am I gonna do with all this?"

"I'm sorry sir but we just can't ship it."

"But you can ship this, right?" The man produced a handgun from the other box. Naturally, the shipping agent stepped back a little. "I gotta send this in to be repaired. Can you ship this? Oh, wait hang on." The man removed the full magazine from the weapon and started to take out the live bullets. He then placed the empty magazine back into the gun and handed it over to the agent.

"Sir, if the gun is already broken, why were you going to ship it back loaded?" the agent asked.

"Thought they might need to test it."

Luckily, the agent knew enough about firearms to inspect the chamber and removed the round the cowboy forgot about.

A lady, with bugs, came into the store one day. Of course, the agent didn't know she had bugs at first. She seemed perfectly lovely. She was short and chipper with a pleasant smile that disarmed everyone in the store. It was only when she began to talk did the agent realize something was a bit off.

"I need to send this to the local university," the lady said. The local university was about five miles down the road so immediately something was strange. Why couldn't she take this parcel herself? Upon closer inspection of the label she had prepared, it was going to the school's biology department. Now it could be dangerous. Was she some sort of crazed animal rights activist sending a bomb?!

"What exactly are you shipping ma'am?" the shipping agent asked. She produced what looked like an empty prescription pill bottle from her handbag and placed it on the counter. The shipping agent was confused. It was only after he got a good, close look at the bottle did he notice something moving.

"Ma'am, what's in the bottle?"

"It's bugs," the lady replied.

"Bugs?"

"Yeah, my house is infested with these little things and I have no idea what they are so I'm sending them off to be identified."

The first question that went through the agent's mind was, "Who cares what they are? Doesn't exterminator gas work on pretty much everything?" But he kept that to himself. "I'm sorry ma'am, but we can't ship these. We can't ship any live animals."

"Oh, really? Ok," she said. The woman then proceeded to unscrew the cap to the bottle. She then stuck her finger inside and began to crush to death each individual insect. Lord only knows what she would have done with a box of kittens. The agent stood back and watched this woman go after each bug for several minutes.

"I'm sorry," she said, "I know I'm taking a long time."

"Oh no, go right ahead" the agent replied. "I've never seen anybody do this before!" After five minutes of squishing, the woman was satisfied she had triumphed over her adversaries and screwed the cap back on. The transaction was processed, she paid, and went on her marry way. "Hey Bernice!" the agent yelled back to his coworker, "You're never going to guess what I need you to pack up."

It was a hot Saturday afternoon and with the air conditioner on the fritz, the day wasn't exactly pleasant to begin with. The simple act of moving was enough to cause a downpour of sweat. Only an incredibly creepy customer would have made the day even worse. Guess what happened!

A man with a strange arrangement of facial hair walked through the door with a white box in hand. It wasn't a beard, it wasn't a goatee, it just seemed as if he had recently gotten into a fight with his razor and lost. As he placed the box on the scale, the contents clanked together in a very characteristic way. It was obvious what was in the box, and poorly packed too.

"Hi! I gotta ship this out," Captain Caveman said.

"Oookay, have you shipped with us before?" the agent asked.

"Oh yeah, a ton of times!" the soul patch replied.

"I see, and what are you shipping?"

"Oh, um… it's just some promotional materials for this thing I've got to do." He nervously scratched his pseudo-beard.

"What kind of 'promotional materials?'"

"It's, uh, it's just some, you know, party favors and some posters and stuff."

"Oh really?" the agent asked and placed the box on the counter in front of the man. The glass inside clanked together loudly. "So what's in the box, sir?"

"Oh that? That's just, um, some figurines for this new client I've got. Hehe!"

"Alright then, would you mind if I take a look inside?" the agent asked.

"No, that's not really necessary, is it?"

"That depends. You do know we can't ship alcohol, right?"

"Oh, it's not alcohol."

"Sir," the agent sighed, "what's in the box?" The weirdy-beard sighed in response.

"Alright," he said, followed by a long pause, "they're organs. A few appendixes, actually."

Understandably, the agent was a little thrown off. "I'm sorry sir, but we can't ship those. They are considered bio-hazardous materials."

"Oh, well, I need to send them out. Some guy bought them from me on eBay."

"Oookay, but we can't ship those."

"Alright, I'll try somewhere else," the man said, took his box of creepy organ jars off the counter, and left.

The most disturbing thing the agent could think of at the time was why someone ordered someone else's worthless organs on eBay. As a little time passed, the disturbing question became why someone had organs in their house to sell on eBay to begin with. The again, the guy being completely crazy *would* explain the facial hair.

The items are not always just dangerous or rare. Sometimes, they are simply bizarre and completely disgusting.

A pleasant elderly woman with a thick Irish accent made her way into the store one sunny morning. In her possession was a piece of wood. Seems simple enough doesn't it? Of course, it wasn't.

"Mornin' young man! I'll need to ship this to California if you wouldn't mind packing it up for me," she said through a big grin.

"Sure thing," the agent said. "What is it?"

"It's a walking stick. It's been handed down through my family for years, every time a man gets retired."

"Ok." The agent took the piece of wood to the back and began to wrap it for packing. There was nothing remarkable to it: it was shaped like a small crutch, unvarnished, and it had a piece in the middle that swiveled back and forth. It didn't look like a very effective cane.

As the agent was packing up the item, Daria, his boss, got bored and wandered to the front of the store and struck up a conversation with the Irish woman. The agent couldn't make out what they were saying while he was packing but he did hear laughter. It got louder. As he was closing up the box, Daria came into the back of the store again wiping tears from her eyes and still chuckling.

"What's so funny?" the agent asked.

"I'll tell you in a minute," she said.

The agent went back into the front to the laughing Irish woman and completely her transaction. She paid with a smile and left. The agent went into the back with the box to where

Daria was still laughing. "Ok, you wanna tell me what's so funny?" the agent asked.

"I'm not sure you're going to want to hear this" she said through laughs.

"Come on, what?"

"Ok, apparently in that woman's family there is a tradition of getting this walking stick when they retire."

"Yeah, she told me that. So?"

"So the joke is that when they retire, they're too old to stand up without help, especially when they're drinking at the bar."

"Ok, that's not that funny."

"Oh, it gets better. You know that piece in the middle that swivels?"

"Yeah." "Well, the walking stick is for the *men* in the family. And when they're drinking, because they are so old at retirement, they have a little trouble controlling, um, their bodily functions. The swivel part makes sure nothing runs down their leg and gets on their shoes."

The agent stared blankly at Daria and then dropped the box. She started laughing again.

"Are you telling me you just let me wrap and pack a *piss stick*?!" the agent yelled. Daria started to cry again. "That's disgusting! I just handled a couple generations of drunken Irish whiz!" Understandably, the agent rushed into the bathroom and began to scrub vigorously, all the while shouting, "Not funny! That was not funny!"

A man in army fatigues came into the store with two large boxes one day. One of them seemed to be leaking what looked like sand. He smelled a little funny.

"Need to ship these out. They're going to the same place," he said.

"Alright, and what's in this first box?" the agent said, motioning to the one on the scale.

"Skulls," the man said with a serious face.

The agent took a step back. "Human?"

The man started to laugh. "No, no they're deer skulls. They're going to a taxidermist."

"Sir, this box weighs about 80 lbs. How many skulls do you have in here?"

"Oh, I'd say about forty or so."

"Ooookay." The agent finished with the box filled with dead animal parts and placed it on the ground behind the counter. Camo-man placed the next box on the scale.

"Alright, what's in here?" the agent asked cautiously.

"Skin."

"Oookay, what's this stuff leaking out of the box?"

"That's salt. Need to preserve this stuff if it's going to be tanned."

"Well if salt is coming out of it, is anything else going to be leaking out of it?"

"It shouldn't," said the man. "I just hosed the things down myself."

"Well," the agent thought, "that explains the smell.

WHO DO YOU KNOW IN ANTARCTICA?

One's perception of geography changes after the first few months in the shipping industry. A person gains a better understanding of international locations and their distance from one another. Knowing that British Columbia is a western province of Canada, and not the section of Columbia where everyone drinks tea and owns a double-decker bus, is something kids in American public schools have a hard time grasping. Being able to distinguish between the multitudes of countries in Asia that now end in "stan" is something even Ivy League students have trouble with. Most importantly, recognizing that "Chad" is the name of the African country the package is going to, and not the name of the recipient, is crucial for not looking like a jackass.

But there are just some places boxes were never meant to tread. For example, I can ship something to Budapest with my eyes closed but it's almost impossible to get a kid's letter to Santa to the actual North Pole. Who is going to sign for it; the elves in the receiving department? If someone's grandfather has decided the revolution is coming and is now hold up "somewhere" in the Australian outback in a fortified bunker, he's not going to get the camouflaged sweater that was knitted for him. Oil rigs in the Bering Sea are generally off the normal delivery route for most drivers. Guards at Area 51 will most likely blow the head off whoever tries to deliver their next shipment of printer toner. Shipping companies do not maintain a fleet of submarines to get care packages of cookies to loved ones in underwater research facilities. And it's probably not a good idea to send a "Wish You Were Here" postcard from a tropical paradise to someone in the frozen wasteland of Siberia. If they got it, which they probably wouldn't, they'd just find the sender and stab them for being a jerk.

Despite the surprisingly vast number of places most shipping companies have never heard of, there is one that is known all too well for its inaccessibility: the dreaded P.O. Box. No one except for the U.S. Post Office can ship to a P.O. Box. Makes sense, doesn't it? After all, it *is* a Post Office Box. When was the last time anyone ever saw a brown, white, or yellow delivery truck idling in front of the post office for a quick delivery? Never, that's when. The Post Office maintains a monopoly on these boxes for the sole purpose that they do get people to use the Post Office. It's quite brilliant. Since they're the government, no one bats an eye to their unfair business practices but everywhere around the country, on a daily basis, poor shipping agents are brutally accosted for being unable to ship to these god-forsaken cubes of aluminum. But where's the logic in that to begin with? The P.O. Box to be delivered to is already *in* a Post Office somewhere which means that's the first stop mail is going to anyway. It stands to reason that sending it thru the Post Office would be the quickest and most logical choice, even if independent shipping companies could deliver to them (which they can't, just to be very, very clear).

A short, fidgety man came in with a long white box one winter day. It was 30 degrees outside and he was in shorts. The fun began quickly.

"Hey, I've gotta get this someplace weird," he said as he looked around the store.

"Ok, have you shipped with us before?" the agent asked.

"No, never."

"Ok, what's your telephone number?"

"Why do you need my number?"

"That's just how we pull up information in the system."

"What if I don't want to give you my number?"

"Then we can't ship your parcel because if something goes wrong, we can't get in touch with you."

"Ok, fine. Here." The man wrote the number down on a piece of paper, folded it, and slid it across the counter to the agent. The agent sighed heavily.

"Alright, where is it going?"

"It's going here, it says it on the box." The man pointed to a few sentences. They read, "To: Dr. Robert Smith, head of Department C. At the end of the dirt road," followed by the town and the zip code.

"Sir, I'm going to need an actual street address" the agent said.

"There is no address."

"What do you mean 'there is no address?'"

"The place, it doesn't exist on any maps."

Thinking that this was some bizarre plot to lure a delivery driver into the woods and kidnap them, the agent got a bit more aggressive in his line of questioning. "Sir, I need to know where this is going or I'm not shipping it. Where exactly is this package going?"

The man mumbled something.

"What?" asked the agent.

"A nuclear power plant," the man repeated.

"Ok, then what's in the box?"

The man didn't answer.

"Sir, if you don't tell me what's in the box I'm going to have to open it."

The man mumbled again.

"Sir, what is in the box?"

"Blow-up doll," the man whispered.

The agent paused. "A what?"

"My brother works at the plant and he's getting married and I'm sending this to him at work as a gag. I just didn't want anyone to know what I was carrying around, you know?" Suddenly, the fidgety aspect came into focus. The shorts were still unexplainable.

"Alright sir, I'm not sure our drivers are going to be able to get this there. Don't you need special clearance to even come close to a power plant?"

"Yeah," the man replied.

"And I'm pretty sure they're going to rip open the box and inspect whatever is being delivered right?"

"I think so."

"So if this is supposed to be a surprise for your brother's bachelor party or something, won't it look kind of bad to his superiors to find him getting a sex toy delivered to work?"

"I never said I liked my brother."

A couple came in one day from far, far away. They seemed perfectly normal. Oh, how foolish the shipping agent was.

"Hiya, we need to ship this package out," the woman said.

"Have you shipped with us before?" the agent asked.

"Nope, never."

"Ok, I'll just need you to fill one of these out." The agent placed a Parcel Shipping Order in front of them and gave them a pen. The man and the woman both dove for the paper and tightly conversed about the proper address the package was going too. After a few minutes, they both came up from the counter and slowly slid the PSO to the agent. He looked at it with a bewildered stare.

"What is this address?" he asked.

"Oh, those are map coordinates," the woman replied.

"I see," said the agent. "Where exactly is this package going?"

"It's going to a small lodge in the Canadian Rockies," the man said.

"Oookay, and what are you shipping?"

"Hot sauce and a hammer."

"I'm sorry, what?"

"Hot sauce and a hammer. Bear meat is very tough and bland."

"Oookay," the agent said and slid the package back towards the customers.

"Hey!" some random guy yelled as he poked his head in the door. "Do you guys send stuff to ships at sea?"

"Come again?" the agent asked.

"My buddy's ship already left port and I need to get something too him."

"I'm pretty sure we can't do that."

"Damn! He left his uniform on my floor!" The man took his head out of the doorway and hurried back to his car.

YOU AND YOUR BOX ARE LEAKING

I will never understand this. No one will ever understand this. Many theories exist as to why people prefer to ship in the rain and the snow and hurricanes and tornadoes and any other freakish form of weather only mentioned in the Bible. No theory has ever held up to scrutiny and so the mystery persists to this day.

One explanation is that when the weather is nice people don't want to hassle with the chore of shipping. They would rather play outside; having barbeques and getting drunk, which I think is a fabulous combination because it increases the odds of an idiot being burned alive. In fact, if trends continue the way they are now, the level of hair gel will steadily increase and clothes will cling tighter to the body. Coupled with already dangerously low I.Q.'s and the inability to think critically outside of a video game scenario, it will become common place for the mouth-breathers of the world to suddenly burst into flames like Gucci-clad Roman candles.

This explanation leads to the idea that people accomplish more when the weather is terrible. They pile up errands until the weather turns and then are forced to dash in every direction to get things done. Heaven forbid they might become moist due to precipitation so they break laws and endanger the lives of fellow civilians to accomplish their past-due goals. These are the people that cause accidents when the weather goes even slightly bad. After all, is it really that hard to drive when it's drizzling?

Perhaps people simply love the smell of wet cardboard. Follow the logic on this one: Most people are stupid. Stupidity is characterized by a below-average I.Q. indicative of poor mental acuity. Maybe they just don't have the synapses firing as fast as they should, who knows. Now, it is entirely possible that the base chemical composition of corrugated cardboard could contain some sort of synaptic trigger, like a pheromone or hallucinogen. Once water is added to the dormant agent, it reacts and becomes active within the cardboard. This mystery agent, once inhaled, could trigger a release of mood elevating hormones in the stupid person's brain by activating their dormant synapses. They feel elated, even giddy, at least more so than stupid people usually feel. However, the high is only temporary and as they come to realize they have more cognitive faculties, they become agitated and short-tempered, angered that they're suddenly wet and holding a smelly box. Smart people don't notice this reaction because all their neurons are firing properly. More over, it's never been studied before because who the hell cares about the atomic properties of cardboard. Then again, perhaps people just like the smell of wet cardboard.

During a particularly heavy storm, a man pulled up in a white pick up truck and parked in the "No Parking" zone in front of the store. He got out, pulled an already soaking box out from the bed of his truck, and came inside. As he walked, his shoes made a squishing sound and he left tiny puddles wherever he stepped.

"Need to ship this," he said as he carried his box over to the scale. Just before he could put the box down, the water-damaged cardboard gave way and the contents of the box spilled out and crashed down on the scale. "Aw shit!" he said and threw down what was left of the dripping box. "That's just fucking great! What the Hell else is going to go wrong today?!" If it had happened as soon as he had said that, it would have been perfect. But unfortunately, it wasn't until the agent had gathered up all the man's things and taken them to the back to be repacked that the other car ran head first into the illegally parked truck.

There was already a foot and a half of snow on the ground when a woman came into the store. She let out a heavy sigh of relief as the door struggled to close behind her in the high winds. As she stepped further inside from the entrance, she shook off a mass of bad weather all over the carpet and began to unwrap herself from the dozens of layers of Inuit-inspired outerwear. After about five minutes of disrobing, she gathered up her belongings and headed up to the counter. She froze in mid-step.

"Damn it!" she yelled out. "I forgot the box!" She quickly rapped herself up like a mummy once more, cursing under her breathe the whole time, and dashed out the door into the blizzard. She made it about three feet before a heavy wind knocked her into a snow bank in the parking lot.

A BOX LIKE A THOUSAND OTHERS BEFORE IT

It's incredibly important to understand that once a driver picks up a package, the control goes from the shipping agent to the massive and all-powerful delivery machine. That's it, game over. A shipping agent has absolutely no control over what happens to that box once it steps outside into the great big world. I can no more absorb the whole of the Atlantic Ocean with my socks then protect a package all the way to its final destination.

Oh sure, it can be packed with great care and professionalism to try and prevent any damage. However nothing is going to save the preciously adorable ceramic pile of crap a customer's A.D.D.-riddled five-year-old spewed out in art class when a loader decides to drop a 200 pound engine block on top of it. If it did manage to survive, then that kid is an engineering genius and should be working for N.A.S.A.

Packages are not protected from the elements. If someone doesn't want items to get wet, they should be wrapped in plastic inside the box because they will most likely be caught in a down pour or dropped in a river or hit with a fire hose. No one in the shipping industry gives a damn about "This Way Up", so don't even waste the time applying the stickers. "Live Cargo" will quickly become dead cargo. Nothing sent for six dollars is going to be refrigerated so unless it's packed in ice, that casserole is rotting on the way to grandma's house.

Most importantly, the word "Fragile" in the shipping industry gets lost in translation a bit. It is best understood as, "If this sticker is anywhere on the package, hurl this box with the force of a thousand locomotives at the nearest concrete wall". It may as well have "Kick Me" written all over the outside.

A man with the remnants of what I believe use to be a box came into the store one morning. He placed the mass of crushed cardboard and miles of tape on the scale and beamed proudly. The box sank slightly under its own weight.

"Need to get this to Ottawa!" he said triumphantly.

The agent carefully poked the heap of scraps. "Oooookay, what's in the 'box?'" the agent asked.

"It's a hot water heater!" he replied, bristling with confidence again.

The agent poked at the mess again. Some tape came loose and a flap popped open. "Sir, this is going to have to go in another box. It'll never survive the trip like this."

His mood suddenly turned. "Oh no! I'm not paying for another box! It took me forever to get this thing packed in the first place! I've shipped these things before to Canada! It just needs a little more tape!" The man produced his own tape gun and proceeded to wrap up the sides with another half inch thick layer. "There!" he said when he had finished, "All it needs now is a fragile sticker! Can you put one of those one for me?"

"Yeah, I can but I don't think it will do much good."

"It'll be fine! Last time I shipped one of these it got totally destroyed but that's because it didn't have a fragile sticker on it!" the man said and began to beam again. The agent's head began to throb but he continued with the sale. The water heater was shipped out, the transaction was paid for, and the man left with a spring in his step.

Three days later, the phone rang. "Yeah, I shipped a hot water heater to Canada a few days ago and it got completely destroyed!" the man yelled into the phone.

"I'm sorry to hear that sir," the agent replied rolling his eyes.

"Yeah, well, it only had *one* fragile sticker on it! If it had more it would have made it! Thanks a lot, dick!" The man hung up. It took a moment for the agent to take in what had just happened, especially since he made sure he didn't bother to waste any fragile stickers on the douche-bag's junkyard box. He wondered where that sticker came from.

Drivers don't hang out at the stores. They don't sit in the back, hoping and praying someone will come in so they can leap into the air and experience the exalted honor of receiving a parcel and escorting it back to the Hub. It doesn't work like that. They've got better things to do. In fact, like every other place that drivers pick up from, there's usually some sort of schedule to follow. Typically, if a store closes at 7:00, the last pick up is going to be somewhere around 6:30 at the latest.

It was a bright, sunny Saturday afternoon in June. The trees swayed gently in the early summer breeze as children laughed and played far too close to the street. A pair of delightful squirrels chased one another among the flowers and people on bicycles darted past the store. It was a beautiful day, and as such, no one had come in since noon.

On Saturdays, the store's hours are from 9 a.m. to 4 p.m. No sense in staying open any longer since the drivers have to be back at the Hub by 5 p.m., making our last pick up at 3:30. It was 3:50. No one had come by in four hours. Taking this as a sign to go enjoy the day, Bernice and the shipping agent decided to close up. The registers were closed and counted, the security gates were pulled and locked, and the lights were turned off. It was 3:57 when *she* arrived.

"Hello?!" she screamed as she pounded on the front door. She was an elderly woman and from the looks of her, a cold-hearted bitch. "I need to ship this!"

Bernice opened the door. "I'm sorry ma'am, but we just closed."

"What?!" the old hag yelled. "It's 3:57! I've still got 3 minutes left! Let me in!"

"I'm sorry ma'am but we're closed. The computers are off. We can't ship anything right now. Besides, it's after our last pick up," Bernice tried to explain.

"But your sign says you're open until 4 o'clock! I should be able to ship this!" The elderly woman tried to push her way in.

"Ma'am! We are closed! We'll be open Monday morning!" Bernice yelled, holding the door firmly in place.

"This is horrible how you're treating me! I'm going to tell your manager about this and get you fired!"

"Go right ahead, ma'am! I still can't ship your package!"

"Oh, go to hell, bitch!" the old lady said and turned for her car.

"Oh *hell* no!" Bernice said and lunged for the woman. Luckily the shipping agent anticipated this reaction and grabbed Bernice before she could slaughter the woman. "Did you fuckin' hear *that* shit?! I oughta lay that dusty old bitch out! Stupid-assed dried-up old fuckin' skank! Hope she chokes on a wrinkled old cock and dies, bitch!"

"That's good, let it out. Find your happy place," the agent said in between fits of laughter.

It was 7:20 p.m., twenty minutes after closing on a Friday night. The shipping agent was cleaning up and getting the place ready for the next day. It had been a long shift: lots of people asking incredibly stupid questions, getting blamed for things that weren't even close to his fault ("Your driver just cut me off in traffic! What the Hell is *your* problem?!"), and dealing with those too foolish to know how to complete the process of taping a box shut. Exhausted, and desperate to head home, the agent pulled the last gate shut and turned off the lights. As he turned to take the garbage out, he heard a knock at the door.

"Hey, I need to ship something," a woman yelled from the other side.

"I'm sorry," the agent replied, "We're closed."

"Can't you just take this one?"

"There's nothing I can do, ma'am. We are closed."

The woman turned in a huff, took out her cell phone, and began screaming. A few moments later, the phone rang. The agent ignored it. It rang again. The same action was taken. Then the agent's cell phone rang. It was the boss. Like an idiot, he picked it up.

"Hello?"

"Hi, it's Daniel. Is there a woman outside your store trying to ship something?"

"Yes, but as you know, and as she's been told, we are closed. I've already shut everything down. There's nothing I can do."

"Bring the computers back up and take her package," the boss said and hung up. Extremely pissed off, the agent let the horrible woman in the store, waited the twenty minutes for the computers to come back up, and took the woman's information.

"Alright, when does your package need to get there?" the agent asked.

"Oh, there's no hurry," she replied.

"If there's no hurry, why couldn't this wait until Monday?"

"I didn't want it in my trunk anymore."

The agent still has fantasies about beating that woman to death with a three-hole punch to this day.

Drivers will not wait for customers, they do not care about customers, and the only people that hate those who ship more are the agents that have to actually have to talk to them. The fine men and women in the big box-like trucks have very focused jobs: they pick up the stuff and they deliver the stuff. That's it. Don't ask them how much it would cost to send a thousand tennis balls to Aruba because they don't know. Hell, I don't even know. These poor folks are out in the blistering cold and unbelievable heat, in what are essentially large, mobile aluminum ovens without ventilation, adhering to an incredibly strict schedule, while battling the same traffic that drives the rest of us crazy all day long. And trust me, the vast majority of drivers are as crazy as a mad cow on crack.

A driver came to do a sweep of the store one evening. The usual driver, Ralph, was nowhere to be seen. This other driver, Steve, was familiar so the agent asked him what had happened to Ralph.

"Yeah, I saw him just this morning. Is he doing another route or something?" the agent inquired.

"Oh, he might not be in for a week or two," Steve said and started to laugh hysterically.

"What's up, Steve?"

Steve composed himself by taking a deep breath. "Alright, you know how Ralph is always talking about hunting and fishing and all that shit?"

"Yeah?"

"Well, he came in this morning as usual, grabbed his deliveries for the morning, and took off on his route. The exit road for the Hub goes along this stretch of woods in the industrial sector. There was this dead deer along the side of the road this morning, big one too. Must have been hit last night or something. Anyway, Ralph gets finished with his deliveries, does his first round of sweeps, and heads back to the Hub to drop them off. He must have gotten the idea during his deliveries this morning because instead of going in the usual entrance, he went around the back way to the exit. He pulled his truck up to the dead deer, got out with his tools, why he had them in his truck already no one can figure out, and started to cut off the deer's head."

The agent stood in stunned silence for a moment. "He did what?"

"I swear to God, dude. He started sawing off the fuckin deer's head! He told the supervisor later that it was a good sized buck and he didn't want to let such a good trophy go to waste."

"What?"

"Here's the fuckin kicker: so Ralph's cutting up this dead deer, right? Right on the side of the road! Then, all of a sudden, a school bus filled with kids starts to go by. They must have been on some field trip or something but as they went by, Ralph looks up, covered in blood, hacksaw in hand, *in uniform*, and waves to the kids, man! They all started screaming like crazy!" Steve burst into laughter again. "So yeah, Ralph's gonna be on suspension for a while!"

STRIKE ME DOWN, O MERCIFUL LORD

Claims... No other word drives as much despair and misery into the very soul of a shipping agent. It signals the beginning of a painful and hopeless process that will leave all parties involved slumped over with an empty shot glass still in hand. Many an agent in the shipping world has lost faith in a higher power because if there truly was a kind and loving God, he wouldn't allow this kind of suffering to happen.

The claims process begins when an item that was shipped arrives damaged or is lost. Unfortunately, the way it is suppose to work is the person who shipped the item calls up the delivery company and informs them of the problem. The receiver then has to hold on to the item until it can be inspected by someone from the company. After inspection, the shipper needs to fill out some paperwork and prove the value of the item in question. Once all the paperwork is done, someone at the company will review the costs and evaluations and determine if payment is applicable and for how much. Finally, the company sends off a check for the amount of the item's worth and the shipper skips off into the sunset towards the land of rainbows and cupcakes. That's how it should work.

More times than not, (who the Hell am I kidding, *every* single time) a pissed-off shipper will call the store the package was sent out of and viciously scream at the poor agent who was foolish enough to let the foul mouthed, shaved ape into the store in the first place. After being blamed for something completely out of their control, the agent will contact the corporate office and inform them of the problem. At this time, the agent will be asked a long list of stupid questions such as, "Would you classify the item as cracked, chipped, halved, or shattered?", "Where packing materials used in the proper manner to insure a safe arrival?", and my personal favorite, "Is the item repairable?" (As if an agent's night job is as an electrical engineer or glass blower. How would *you* know if Grandpa's new nebulizer is repairable?!) To all these questions, the agent will have absolutely no idea, thus wasting everyone's time. Once this pointless conversation is over, the agent now has to inform the irate customer who verbally bashed them earlier that an inspector will go out to check the damage of the item at the receiver's location. This is where 90% of all claims come to a screeching halt.

There will always be something wrong on the receiver's end. The shipper may not have their phone number and cannot contact them to inform them of the inspection. The receiver may have thrown away the original packaging thereby making it impossible to tell if it was improperly packed. The inspector may not be able to gain access to the item because the receiver won't let them in. The problem may even be that after informing the shipper that the item was broken, they just decided to ship it back to its origin and cross their fingers that a shiny, new replacement is on its way. Despite whatever happens, the agent who originally processed the package will be blamed. "What the Hell do you mean the receiver opened fire on the inspector and led the police on a seven state high-speed pursuit and the item has been impounded as evidence and no one is allowed to view it until the trial?! Why haven't you inspected it yet?!"

If by some miracle the inspector does manage to take a look at the item and determines that it was damaged during transit and, more rarely, it was the company's fault, the shipper has been truly blessed. But as the old saying goes, be careful what you wish for. The shipper is more than likely to be bitten in the ass in the stages to come.

What is needed at this point is proof of the item's worth. The shipping agent now has to inform the belligerent customer that invoices, receipts, or any documentation that shows the company how much an item is worth is needed to complete the process. The agent will be chewed-out again, this time blamed for not telling the customer that such paperwork was necessary (despite it being one of the first things they were told) and that the company should just pay them whatever they declared as its value. However, the shipping company is not entirely stupid and will probably know that Last Supper kitchen place mats are probably not worth the four thousand dollars claimed as insurance.

Supposing the loud-mouth does find some sort of legitimate receipt for the item in question, and not something they cut and pasted together in PhotoShop, then the information will be sent over to the company for review. And now the grueling process of waiting for a reply begins. During the next few weeks and months, the agent will be harassed, threatened, and lambasted nearly everyday. "Where the *fuck* is my money! I did what you asked me to do! Why the Hell is this taking so damn long! I shit faster than this and I ain't got no colon!" No excuse will be accepted and no attempt to calm the customer will be successful. There is only one thing that will stop this annoying and brutal assault and that is a check. Of course, that check will most likely turn the annoyance into a crazed maniac.

Let's say that the shipper does get compensation for the item that was damaged. The proud day arrives when they get the call that their check is waiting at the store and they can pick it up any time. They have beaten a mighty corporation and struck a blow for justice everywhere. Finally, the little guy gets his reward. As the shipper steps through the doorway, head held high and chest puffed out, they know that through all the hardships and obstacles, they have made it. The agent will hand them their check and the moment will be glorious and triumphant before they open the envelope with their name on it containing the spoils of their war. At this point, the agent starts to pray they just take the damn thing home and open it there.

They never do. The shipper opens the envelope. The sound of the paper tearing is the same sound of their universe being ripped apart. It is then that they realize they haven't won and, indeed, they've been screwed.

"What the fuck?!" the shipper will exclaim in an octave usually reserved for dogs. "A hundred bucks?! You people smashed my ten thousand dollar stereo, took nearly a year torturing me with your damn excuses and paperwork, and all I get is a hundred bucks?!" It will only get worse from there. The agent will be pummeled with insults ranging in everything from their suppose incompetence in the workplace to the virtue of their mother. A stable agent will try to calm the assailant and explain the situation to them, assuring them that they had

nothing personally to do with the damage or the decision and they have no control over what happens to a box once it leaves the store. An unstable agent will leap across the counter and beat the living shit out of the guy who just cracked wise about their momma (I've seen it happen). At the end of the day, someone may be in jail, someone may be getting drunk, but no one is happy thanks to the claims process.

It has become clearer to me over time that no one in this world can call themselves "sane". Everyone's at least a little bit crazy. Having a slightly screwed up mind is really the only way to insure survival in a society as dysfunctional as ours. Bizarre rituals, twisted ideas, and horribly skewed beliefs offer a mental air bag to the daily 30 car pile-up that is American life.

For example, a co-worker of yours gets the boss to dump an extra load of work on you by telling them you're a "specialist" in that kind of task. What makes it worse was that you got assigned this crap before your regular morning coffee with cream and two sugars, each stirred in separately. The usual fantasy of crushing their skull under the lid of the copy machine dances through your mind until you're belief structure kicks in and you say to yourself, "They'll get theirs in Hell". You have just dealt with a backward situation, in which a supposed ally turned against you by making you look "good", that interrupted your bizarre ritual, by imagining their gruesome demise and trusting an invisible deity will somehow smite them. Sounds pretty crazy to me.

The problem is not that people are crazy, that's inevitability. The problem is the level of crazy a person shares with the world. When someone "snaps", it's really not a pleasant time to be around them. Unfortunately, for many the perfect time to lose one's marbles is when they try to ship.

It happens more frequently then one might think; an over-stressed business man or woman rushes in to complete a complex shipping task, where these forms need to go here and these forms need to go there but those forms need to be notarized first and then re-routed to a second destination... A father or mother with three hyperactive children screaming and tearing up the store is just trying to get in touch with the receiver but they've moved and they can't find the right address... A hard working laborer who spent the week getting yelled at and eventually fired has been fighting with the state for the paperwork for their divorce and payments for child support that needed to be shipped yesterday... You can feel the tension around them. The stench of dried flop sweat and the worn lines of pressure across their face signal that their crack-up is imminent. Of course *these* people are going to lose it. It's the ones that saunter in, smiling and whistling, that scare the shit out of you when they go nuts.

It was early in the morning. Beads of dew glistened gently in the rising sunlight as the spring flowers stretched towards the sky to take in the light. The computers had just started to come to life and the fluorescent lights had warmed up enough to hum. It was a promising start to the day... and then he walked in.

He looked sane enough. He wore brown loafers with a pair of khaki cargo shorts and a tee shirt that informed the reader that he had eaten something of significance at a barbeque establishment. In his right hand was a non-descript briefcase. His hair was slightly disheveled and he had a small growth of stubble but he smiled as he moved and nodded a greeting as he came through the door. He was like any other business man who had just had a few days off and remembered he needed to get some stuff done before he went back into the office. As he placed his briefcase on the counter, he leaned in and whispered to the agent behind the desk, "Can you keep a secret?" Things were about to go weird.

"I'm with the F.B.I. and I'm working on a big undercover case right now," the crazy man said nonchalantly. "I was hoping you could help me, and your country, with something."

"Oooookay..." the shipping agent said.

"I need some business cards made up that say I own an auto body shop in Elizabeth, NJ. Can you do that for me?"

"Alright."

"It's part of a really big operation. Yep, been working with the A.T.F. and Homeland Security on this one for a few years and we've almost got the guys were after. Of course, I can't say anymore. Classified."

"Sure thing, sir."

"You see, there's this gang of car thieves from Hungry that have been terrorizing local delivery drivers up and down the East Coast. We've set it up so they think I'm repairing a fleet of bread delivery trucks."

"That's, um, really great sir. How many cards do you need?"

"Oh, just one."

"You only need one business card?"

"Yep, it's for the big boss."

"Sir, we generally sell them by the hundred."

"Then I'll pay for a hundred but only give me one."

"Oooookay…"

The shipping agent went back to work preparing the business cards as the crazy man kept going on about bread trucks and international windshield bandits. It seemed as though it took forever but the agent finally got the job done and charged the man for his card.

"This is great! They will totally buy this! You've done a great service for America. You should be proud," the whack-job said and turned for the door. He got about three steps away before he stopped suddenly and stared at the business card intently. The agent thought that he had done something wrong at first but after five minutes of silence the agent began to think that man was having some sort of stroke. After ten minutes of just standing in the middle of the store, gazing at a business card, it got a little creepier. After fifteen minutes, the agent was unsure about whether they should call someone to do something. Luckily the awkward stillness was broken when the man suddenly tore up the card frantically and started to sob and scream. No one knew what to do as this man fell to his knees and bawled his eyes out. After a minute or so he suddenly stood up, wiped his face clean, pulled a cell phone out of his pocket and continued for the door. As he was heading out, the agent heard the man say, "Hello, St. Mary's Mental Hospital? Hi, I'd like to commit myself again." Of course, the agent thought this was a practical joke. "This guy must be just messing with us," the agent thought as he watched the man hang up his phone and sit down on the curb outside the store. It took about ten minutes before an ambulance that said "St Mary's" on the side pulled up, threw a blanket around the man, and carted him off. "Huh, that's a pretty good joke," the agent thought.

A college student came into the store one cold evening. She seemed a little frazzled but it was about time for finals so it was understood. Her hair was tangled and disheveled, she looked as though she hadn't slept or changed her clothes in a few days, and her smell seemed to support that impression. She walked with a glazed-over stare in her eyes. In her arms she clutched a pile of papers.

"Hi, can I help you?" the shipping agent asked. Her eyes went from glassed-over to razor-like focus.

"*Fuuucckkkk!*" she screamed for a few seconds and then was quiet, except for her labored panting. The agent just stood there wishing he had a can of pepper spray or something underneath the counter. Her hands slapped against her forehead hard enough to be clearly audible. "I, I forgot the address at home. Fuck!" she yelled again. She was now on the verge of tears.

"It's ok," the agent tried to reassure her, "maybe I can help you. Are you shipping that out?" the agent asked pointing at the papers in her frantic grasp.

"Yes, I need to get this out and I've been working on it for days and I need it to go to my professor up at Northwestern but I can't remember the address and I haven't slept in three days and I... I..." She spoke in an incredibly high pitch at thousand words a minute.

"It's ok. I can pack that up for you and get your information at least. Is there anyone you can call for the address?" the agent asked.

"No! No one is here! Everyone left for the break and I'm the only one here and I need to get this out!" she screeched.

"Ok! I can hang on to this here while you go get the address."

"*No!*" she yelled and turned away with the papers like a child protecting their favorite toy. "I can't leave it with you! It's too important and if I don't get this to Chicago by tomorrow morning I'm going to loose my scholarship!" She started to cry. "*Fuucckkkk!*" she yelled out again.

"Ooookay. You still have time to get it out today. The driver won't be here for another hour."

"Can't you look up their address?!"

"No, I can't."

"Why not?! This is the *Post Office* for God-sake!"

"Actually, it's not." The crazed co-ed looked around for a moment.

"Oh shit, then where the Hell *am* I?!" she said and then bolted out the door.

A shaky man came through the door one day, a few times. He stepped through the door, then exited, checked the sign, poked his head in the doorway, went back out, and finally made the long trip over the threshold. He looked around quickly, caught sight of the shipping agent, and put on a hugely scary smile.

"Hello there!" he said, "Need to ship something somewhere."

"Alright, have you shipped with us before?" the agent asked.

"Yes."

"Ok, can I get your phone number?"

"No."

"I'm sorry?"

"I'm not giving you my phone number."

"Oh, it's ok sir. That's just how we look up your information in our database. Nobody's going to call you at home."

"You're not getting my phone number!"

"Sir, if you don't give me your number, you can't ship with us."

"Oh *I* see how it is! You know I need to send something out so you use this opportunity to start a file on me, is that it?!"

"What?"

"Sure, it starts with my number and pretty soon you've got my social security number and my bank cards and then I take the fall for some crime, is that it?! Don't think I don't know what's going on! As soon as you give out one piece of your information, they can find out everything about you! Well I'm sure as Hell not going to fall for it!"

Now that it was confirmed the agent was dealing with a complete nutcase, he decided to have a little fun. "Sir, who is 'they?'" the agent asked.

"The corporations! They can't get access to government records on people until they willing give up some part of their person information!"

"Sir, that's not what happens. If we really needed to know more about you, we'd simply lift your DNA from your fingerprints on your package."

The crazy guy's eyes went wide. "What?" he asked.

"Sure, it's not hard" said the agent, "All we need to do is dust for your print and then lift it with some special tape we have in the back. Why do you think we use both clear *and* brown 'packing' tape?" The agent made quotation gestures.

The man started to lose it. He backed away from the counter very slowly, his hands clearly visible in front of him. As he stepped away, he bumped into another customer just entering the store. He turned to her and said, "Don't give them anything!" and then darted out the door.

OF ALL THE CRAZY, BACKWARD-ASSED IDEAS...

Not too long ago, in a land made of fairy tale wishes and potent LSD, a wise old wizard in a three-piece suit gazed out the window of his enchanted penthouse office. His mind was troubled by slowing profit trends in the far off kingdom of Accounting. He consulted the mystical fairies of Research and Development but they had not the answers he sought. It was only after he had faced the dreaded demon known as Sobriety, and did battle wielding the blazing swords of Cocaine and Wood Varnish, did he have a vision: Shipping... and Photo Copies! *Of course!* It makes absolute, perfect sense to put those two things together! And so it was that people would come to equate interstate commerce with badly-colored prints of missing dog flyers. The magical land of Poorly-Thought-Out-Enterprises was at peace once again.

Printing and shipping have nothing to do with one another. Nothing. *Nothing!* Customs invoices and maybe a stray shipping manifest is all the paperwork that the shipping industry would ever need to copy. But *oh* no, some brilliant M.B.A. with no practical experience whatsoever had to pipe up at a meeting and say, "You know fellas, boxes are made from cardboard, and cardboard is kinda like paper, and stuff gets printed on paper... Gasp! Shipping and copies! Quick, call the Vatican! It's divinely inspired!" After that, it wasn't enough that shipping agents be able to get a package to the other side of the world within twenty four hours. Now that package had to be full color, double sided, landscape oriented, booklet bound, cut-to-bleed, and five millimeter laminated before it was jammed in a box and kicked out the door.

I never really wanted to know how to coil bind something. It's just not a skill I use on a daily basis. It never occurred to me that my life might be richer and more fulfilling if I knew how to 10-up a business card for easier printing and cutting. Most of all, the tranquil zen of trimming thousands upon thousands of pieces of lamination so they look neat and straight never pushed me over the edge so far as to contemplate laminating my airways shut and welcoming in the sweet release of oblivion. Combining shipping and printing has made my life fuller because there is nothing more rewarding that postponing the work I am suppose to do to deal with neurotic sociopaths all day in an over-exerted effort to make ten cents on a sale.

The actual work itself isn't atrociously terrible. Sure, it's a pain in the ass to hand collate a hundred business proposals but it can be done. But just like in shipping, it is the people that make life miserable for any printer. They ask for outrageously ridiculous tasks to be performed in unrealistic time periods (i.e. "I need 40,000 wedding invitations printed on paper made from plants grow in the Brazilian rainforest and processes by indigenous eunuchs with over-bites in the next three minutes"), just like shipping. They want their crap produced within the tolerance of a few microns and be able to withstand the horrors described in the Book of Revelations (i.e. "I'm going to be doing my stockholder presentation in a room without air conditioning so can you make sure the lamination is thick enough to survive a drop in a volcano? Oh, but it can't feel *too* thick"), just like shipping. They will ask the dumbest, most excruciatingly stupid questions imaginable (i.e. "I know this is printed in black and white but if I copy it on the *color* copier, it will come out in color, right?"), just like shipping. And they will throw the most vicious hissy-fit if something doesn't come out exactly as they had imagined in their wildest printing fantasies (i.e. "This shade of blue doesn't *exactly* match the blue I gave you! I know because I took it to some sort of color specialist and after yelling at him for an hour he told me I was right!"), just like shipping.

An incredibly creepy man came into the store one day with a file folder under his arm. Despite the fact that it was May, he wore a long black trench coat and a bright red scarf. Topping off the ensemble was a black beret and a couple layers of foundation pasted to his face. He approached the counter and leaned in. The shipping agent leaned way back.

"I... need to make a few color copies, young man" the creepy old man said in a way the agent had only heard coming from bad Hannibal Lecter impressions. The agent took a look at what he needed printed and was quite disturb to see that they were all pictures of either priests or young children. The agent felt the hairs on the back of his neck stand up as he walked over to the copier and began copying each photo.

A moment or two later, the creepy man walked over slowly and stood right behind the agent, at a distance that wasn't touching but definitely violated personal space requirements. Occasionally, the creepy man would say things like, "That copy is a good one," or "You're really... skilled at this, aren't you young man?" thereby making the agent shudder in horror. Finally, he came across a picture of the creepy man himself, a few years younger and dressed as a priest. Now the agent was getting worried.

The agent finished the copies and rushed back behind the counter. He rang up the creepy man as fast as he could in a desperate effort to get him the Hell out of the store. While he was putting the totals in the register, the creepy man said, "I... love your hair. It's such a... magnificent... shade of blonde. Is that your... natural color?"

"Um, sure," the agent said without looking up.

"I wish I... had hair like yours."

The agent winced, really expecting that sentence to end with the name Clarisse. "Ooookay, your total is $3.75."

"What a bargain. I'll... have to come back with more." The creepy man paid what he owed, gave the agent a terrifying wink, and left. It took all the composure the shipping agent had not to sprint to the back of the store and throw up.

The next day, creepy man was back. This time, his hair was dyed bright blonde. The shipping agent saw the pervert coming and nonchalantly slipped a box cutter into his pocket just in case he was kidnapped and had to escape a basement dungeon. At the same time, he took off for the back of the store.

"Hey Daria," he said to his boss, "would you mind taking care of this guy that's coming in? He is creepy as Hell and I'd really rather not get eye-raped by him again."

"Sure, I got it," she said and made her way to the front. Daria greeted the creepy man, took his copies over to the machine, and got to work. It was a few moments before another customer came in and, since there was no one else to help them, the agent had to step out of the back room and take care of them. The transaction went smoothly and after the customer had paid and left, the agent was finishing up with the box. It was then that the creepy man came over and said, "Perhaps I could... pay this young man to come back to my place and... take a look at it."

The shipping agent shot up to attention and reached for the box cutter in his pocket. *"What?!"* he yelled.

"I just... can't seem to figure out what's wrong... with my fax machine. I thought you might be able to take a look at it. Surely a bright... young... man like you knows of these things."

"Sir, I don't do that. Call the company's help line."

"But I live... just down the street. Money is no object."

The shipping agent felt as though he had just been called a prostitute. His grip around the cutter tightened. "That's not my job. Find someone else," the agent said through clenched teeth.

About that time, the agent looked over at his boss only to see her bent in half and struggling to breathe since she had been laughing so hard. Tears were running down her face. The agent hurried to the back of the store and spent the next few minutes dry heaving.

A pick-up truck filled with boxes pulled up in front of the store on a Saturday afternoon. Two men jumped out, came into the store, and asked if they could use the hand truck. The shipping agent handed them the truck and they proceeded to bring in wave after wave of boxes.

"Ok," said the agent when they had brought everything inside, "where do these need to be shipped?"

"Oh, we don't need them shipped," said one of the men, "All of the documents in these boxes need to be copied."

The agent looked at the mountain of papers and shuttered. "Ok, but it's going to be at least a week to get all this done."

"That's fine. They just have to be done *exactly* as they are now. Just call us when we can pick it all up." Before the agent could ask the men the little details, like, "What is your phone number so we can tell you when the Colossus of Collation is finished?" they were out the door, in their truck, and down the road. And so the agent was left with the towering mass of legal documentation that need to be sorted through and copied (this type of litigation is generally the most despised in the printing world and is referred to as "shit-igation").

Hours passed by, and then days. Box after box, file after file, and page after page had to be sorted through one by one. The monotony of removing one staple from two pieces of paper, or a paper clip from three, copying the pages, and then replacing the staple or paper clip on the originals, wore down the will and resolve of the shipping agent. It took six days of copying in unfathomably long shifts to complete the process. For days afterwards, the agent had nightmares about staple removers biting him repeatedly as the incessant hum and beep of the printer mocked his pain. The smell of toner never truly came out of his clothes.

It wasn't until nearly a week after completion that the men came back to retrieve their copies. They marveled at how their impressive pile of useless information had doubled in size and joked about the best way to move the mound.

"Alright," said one of the men, "let's tape them up and get them ready to move out." They produced tape guns and proceeded to seal the boxes.

"Whoa! You don't even want to see if we did the job right?" the agent asked.

"No need," said one of the men without looking up from the tape, "the originals are off to the incinerator and the copies are headed back into the basement to take their place."

The agent stood stunned. All that effort, all that horribly tedious work had been for nothing. Naturally, he was a little pissed off. "This job took forever! Why did you need copies then? What was wrong with the originals?"

"They were starting to smell a little funny. Hell, they've been in that basement for at least thirty years!"

COMPLETELY RANDOM STUPIDITY

There are times (many, many times), when a powerful idiocy makes its presence known in the blink of an eye. It is as if the doorway to the store is a magical portal that gives off some exotic radiation, turning all who cross its threshold into drooling nimrods. For as long as I have worked in the shipping industry I have witnessed this phenomenon, almost on a daily basis. It is this sudden burst of stupidity, this totally inexplicable thrust of utter dementia that will continue to haunt my dreams long after I have left this world. Here is just an incredibly small sample of some of the insanely moronic questions I have encountered working behind the box:

- "Do you guys ship things here?"
- "I have this package for the Post Office. Can I drop it off here?"

- "Are you guys open?"
- "This needs to go Next Day. When will it get there?"
- "Do you guys take food stamps?"
- "The sign out front says 'Open 8 a.m. to 7 p.m.' Are those your hours?"
- "Do you have any tape?"
- "Do you have any boxes?"
- "Can I borrow some tape?" (as if they were going to give it back later)
- "I'm trying to find your store. How close am I?" (over the phone)
- "If you're not open on Sundays, can I still take my package to the Post Office?"
- "Can this go like this?" (placing a loaded rifle on the counter)
- "One of your delivery drivers left this notice on my door a few minutes ago. Can I pick up my package here?"
- "What would this cost if I sent it through the Post Office?"
- "Does this need to face up or down inside the box?"
- "How do I find my package if it never gets there?"
- "How come you don't wear those cool shorts?"
- "I need to send this but it's not money. Is that ok?"
- "Can you make sure no one stacks any other boxes on top of mine on its way to Russia?"
- "What's the best way to ship a hundred pounds of raw meat?"
- "Where is the nearest store owned by your competition?"
- "Can this go like this?" (placing a box missing three sides on the counter)

- "Where is Tempe Arizona?"
- "I need to make sure this address is right. What's the time in Japan?"
- "Can the delivery driver leave my package at the back door of the neighbor's house and call me to let me know it was sent next door?"
- "My package came broken. Do you fix it here?"
- "How will the delivery driver know where my package is going?"
- "At exactly what time will my package be delivered?"
- "You guys must ship a lot of stuff, huh?"
- "My package will go out today, right?" (first customer of the day)
- "Can this go like this?" (placing a plastic sandwich bag of shampoo on the counter)
- "If you buy fireworks out of state, can you ship them here?"
- "What do you intend to do about the rude driver I just encountered?"
- "How come I never get junk mail from you guys?"
- "I need a box that's 18 feet long and an inch and a half wide. You guys carry that, right?"
- "What kind of gas mileage does one of your delivery trucks get?"
- "My package had a 'Fragile' sticker on it and it still arrived broken! How come?"
- "Do I sign this form where it says, 'Customer Signature'?"
- "Do I put down my information where it says, 'Sent From'?"
- "Well, if the people I was shipping to don't live there anymore, why didn't you just forward it to their new address?"

- "Do I write where it needs to go under the section that says, 'Send To'?"
- "I don't know how to say where my package is going in English so I'm going to write the address in Chinese. Is that ok?"
- "Where can I get one of those things to stick on to the other thing so I know that the thing wasn't placed with any other things?"
- "Do you ship drugs?"
- "How come you guys don't wear hats?"
- "I'm sending this birthday gift to my niece in Nebraska. Do you think she'll like it?"
- "How would you pack the exhaust system for a 1973 Ford Thunderbird?"
- "I tracked my package on your website and it said my package was delivered. Can you track it for me?"
- "My package was delivered broken! Why did you do that?!"
- "Who do I talk to about kickin' my delivery driver's ass?!"
- "When I shipped my package, I accidentally gave you the wrong address. How come my package wasn't delivered?"
- "If I ship something during a Leap Year, will it still get there on time?"
- "Your website said there was a train derailment and my package got damaged. Why did you do that?"
- "I didn't mean to send my package to that destination. Can I get a refund?"

- "The person I'm shipping to won't be home until 3 a.m. Is there a way to get it to him at that time?"
- The Stupidest Question Ever Asked: "Is there a Store X around here?" (asked while standing inside of Store X and speaking with a shipping agent wearing a shirt that says "Store X")

The End

About the Author

Joseph Willish survived tragedy, near death experiences, and the horrors of Hurricane Katrina only to have his soul crushed under the weight of styrofoam packing peanuts in the shipping industry. He currently lives in North Carolina where he spends his time shaking in the corner of a small room and yelling at squirrels.